grasses

THE ROYAL HORTICULTURAL SOCIETY

Roger Grounds

grasses

choosing and using these ornamental
plants in the garden

Special photography
Andrew Lawson

Quadrille

Editorial Director Jane O'Shea
Art Director Helen Lewis
Project Editor Carole McGlynn
Art Editor Paul Welti
Photography Andrew Lawson, Sarah Cuttle
Production Rebecca Short, Vincent Smith

First published in 2005 by Quadrille Publishing Limited

Cataloguing-in-Publication Data: a catalogue record for
this book is available from the British Library.

ISBN   1-84400-159-8
Printed and bound in Hong Kong

Half title page (page 1): *Pennisetum thunbergii* 'Red
Buttons' (syn. *P. massaicum* 'Red Buttons'); title page
(pages 2–3): *Cortaderia selloana* 'Sunningdale Silver'
in frost; this page (right): *Hordeum jubatum* with
Echinops ritro

Where a grass in the Gallery of Grasses has ♀ after its
name, it has been given the Royal Horticultural Society's
Award of Garden Merit. To achieve this, it must be
excellent for ordinary garden use, reasonably easy to
grow, readily available and not especially prone to pests
and diseases.

Contents

the story of grasses

Since the dawn of mankind grasses have provided us with our staple diet and many other needs but it is only recently that they have come into our gardens as ornamentals. Only now are they appreciated for the translucency of their fragile but enduring flowers, their purity of line and their unique texture, the way they change through the seasons and move with the wind, the ease with which they fit in with other flowers as well as with the natural world beyond our gardens.

At rest or play, ornamental grasses can, more than most plants, calm the mind and delight the senses.

Grasses are the key plants of contemporary gardening, treasured for the luminosity of their flowers, their unique line and texture, their sound and movement, and for their extraordinarily long season of interest. Fluid and dynamic, they fit easily into our gardens, mixing well with other plants. These qualities put them in the forefront of a move towards greater naturalness in gardens.

how grasses came into our gardens

Grasses, for all their current popularity, were slow to come into our gardens. The first grasses to be cultivated were grown for their grains, providing the staple diets of virtually every society: wheats, ryes and barleys in Europe, maize in the Americas, millets in Africa and rice in Asia. Other grasses provide the forage on which meat and dairy animals graze, sugars to sweeten our foods and starches for alcohol. Bamboos, which are true grasses, although beyond the scope of this book, can provide, in warm climates, for almost every need from the cradle to the grave, from building materials to over a thousand manufactured articles.

Beyond that, grasses were seen, like the rest of the natural world, as a threat to our tenuous hold on civilization. So long as the essence of gardening was to assert man's mastery over the natural world, grasses – as the most dominant plants in almost every part of the globe – were unwelcome, and gardens, to assert man's domination of nature, had to be as different as possible from the vegetation beyond their bounds. But aesthetics follow ethics, and now that the natural world is seen as our friend rather than our enemy, and ecology is the ethic of the moment, we can allow the natural world back into our lives, and can create gardens not alien to, but in harmony with, the indigenous flora. And since more plants on earth are grasses than plants of any other kind, they are essential to any attempt at gardening in a natural idiom, though they can be used equally well in formal and even contrived gardens. For gardens should not be confused with the natural world. Gardens are only gardens because we intervene – and the grasses were always there.

A few grasses, such as Job's tears (*Coix lacryma-jobi*), were grown in monastery gardens, the hard seeds sometimes used for making rosaries, while several are mentioned in the old herbals, which were more about useful plants than about specifically healing ones. Gerard, for example, in his *Herball* (1597) included couch grass which he said was useful for healing 'green wounds', and meadow grass, which apparently has the capacity to 'glew and consolidate together new and bleeding wounds', while the roots of the common reed could be used to draw forth thorns and splinters.

CLASSIFICATION

As long ago as the third century BC, Theophrastus (*c.*370–*c.*287BC) realized that grass seeds germinate with a single seed leaf, while those of most other plants germinate with two seed leaves. This was the beginning of a classification system. Little further progress was made until 1704, when John Ray published a key separating grasses from sedges (though he did include cat-tails, *Acorus* and ginger among the grasses). The great Carl Linnaeus (1707–78) finally brought order to the plant world with his sexual system of classification, recognizing the grasses as a distinct group. But it was Bernard de Jussieu (1699–1777) who, in his more natural system of classification, gave grasses the status of a family, which he named Gramineae.

Modern usage, however, requires that plant families take the name of the first genus in that family to be described, and since there is no genus *Gramineum*, the family is now called Poaceae, from the genus *Poa*. Modern systems of classification no longer rely on gross morphological characteristics but rather on DNA analysis which, interestingly, reveals quite different evolutionary relationships between the grasses from those previously considered.

FIRST ORNAMENTAL GRASS

Ornamental gardening as such did not begin until the seventeenth century, and the first nursery listing of a grass specifically as an ornamental occurs in John Kingston Galpine's catalogue of 1782. Galpine was a nurseryman, a native of Blandford in Dorset, England, and the plant is an English native – feather grass (*Stipa pennata*), grown for its long, showy, feathery awns. A century later, William Robinson (1838–1935) was listing nearly 30 ornamental grasses in his classic book, *The English Flower Garden* (1883). By that time a dozen or so grasses were common currency in English gardens, though it seems they were grown more as curiosities than for their beauty, and usually in isolation in the midst of sweeping lawns.

The first grasses to come into our gardens were the weed-like ancestors of the grain crops, such as wheat, which now support almost all people on earth and which are today grown on a vast scale around the world.

ENGLISH RETICENCE

In retrospect, William Robinson's influence has been enormous, for he is in many ways the founding father of the naturalistic trends in gardening which have come to the fore in the last half-century. From a humble background in Ireland, Robinson soon moved to England where he rose to become probably the most influential gardener of his generation. Born with an awkward and argumentative personality, he was forever at war with the established tastes of his time and expounded his views in numerous books and in the many publications he both wrote for and edited. His central quarrel was with what he saw as the mindless patterns of carpet bedding so popular in Victorian times. Long before ecology and habitat became familiar terms to gardeners, Robinson was proposing that good gardens are made by using plants suitable for the site rather than by following an aesthetic ideal. In his seminal book, *The Wild Garden* (1870), he suggested that plants, native and exotic, should be grown 'under conditions where they will thrive without further attention'. This was the tipping point in a longer process beginning with the English landscape style of garden. It rejected the high art of Renaissance gardens and developed, through William Morris, John Ruskin and the Arts and Crafts movement, into the eco-naturalistic trends still gathering force today in reaction to the over-urbanization of most people's lives.

CONTROVERSY

Robinson's contemporary Reginald Blomfield (1856–1942), who was no plantsman, advocated in *The Formal Garden in England* (1892) that gardens should be essentially architectural to provide a suitable setting for the house. Robinson took issue with this and out of the controversy which ensued, arose the Edwardian garden in which 'naturalistic' planting was contained within the geometry of formality, a style of gardening largely derived from partnership of Gertrude Jekyll and the young architect Edwin Lutyens.

Gertrude Jekyll originally trained as a painter, learning watercolour techniques from Hercules Brabazon. In middle life she was forced to abandon painting because of severe and progressive myopia and turned instead to gardening, to which she applied her painterly sense of colour. Her partnership with Edwin Lutyens led to a series of gardens which set the style for a generation and became a key part of the English tradition. Gertrude Jekyll was specific about the placing of grasses in a garden. In the early twentieth century she was advocating the use of large grasses such as pampas, which she called *Gynerium argenteum*, miscanthus, which she called *Eulalia japoncia*, and the provencal reed, which she called *Arundo phragmites*, close to water. She used blue lyme grass (then *Elymus arenarius*) in soft borders of blue and grey foliage with pink and white flowers, and the common woodrush (*Luzula sylvatica*) as ground cover in woodland.

Both Robinson and Jekyll were influential in America at a time when ornamental gardening was gaining status and popularity. This was largely

Helictotrichon sempervirens was much favoured by Miss Jekyll in her borders for its dense, rounded mounds of silver-blue.

Gertrude Jekyll frequently used grasses to give substance and structure to her carefully colour-schemed borders, as seen here in the garden at Hestercombe in Somerset, England.

because American plant hunters had started introducing ornamentals, rather than merely economic plants. Miscanthus and pampas grasses were particularly popular, their scale fitting in well with large American landscapes, but many smaller grasses were also introduced at this time. Yet even while the plant hunters scoured the world to find exotics with which to decorate American gardens, one or two Americans were looking around themselves, stunned by the beauty of their own flora.

THE NATURALISTIC MOVEMENT IN AMERICA

The native gardening movement in the USA was born in the Midwest, where grasses abound, at the heart of the vanishing prairie. Danish-born landscape architect Jens Jensen (1860–1951), working out of Chicago, was perhaps the first landscape architect fully to appreciate the beauties of the Midwest's vast horizons and native plants, and to advocate their use in man-made landscapes. He developed, with the architect Frank Lloyd Wright, the 'prairie style' of landscape gardening. Jensen himself designed parks and gardens using native prairie flora, and his 77-acre Lincoln Memorial Garden in Springfield, Illinois, is planted entirely with Midwest natives.

The American naturalistic gardening movement is quite different from anything known in Europe, largely because in America a hundred years ago true wilderness still existed (and perhaps still does), whereas in Europe every inch of

The 'new wave' gardens of Wolfgang Oehme and James van Sweden marry Karl Foerster's ideas with the American love of wilderness to produce stylized prairies, as seen in this garden beside Chesapeake Bay.

land has been farmed or managed or trampled over for hundreds of years. The American Romantic–philosophical relationship with the wilderness has its roots in the poetry of William Wordsworth, the poetry and writings of Ralph Waldo Emerson and in Henry David Thoreau's *Meditations on Walden Pond*.

But just when the influence of Jens Jensen's prairie style was gathering force, it petered out and the prairies themselves were swept aside by the durum wheats introduced from Russia by Mark Carleton. These increased agricultural production from 60,000 to 20,000,000 bushels a year. From the 1930s onwards, grasses inexplicably disappeared from American gardens so that by the 1950s it was virtually impossible to buy an ornamental grass anywhere in the United States. Fortunately matters were different in Europe at that time.

CONTINENTAL DRIFT

In Europe, where William Robinson is still regarded as the originator of natural gardening, others have developed his ideas along more scientific and ecologically sound ideas. Among these was Willy Lange (1864–1941) of Germany, who, borrowing from both Robinson and Goethe, saw the garden as an extension of the native vegetation, specifically advocating German plants for German gardens set in a German landscape, an approach which anticipates the modern idea of the garden as a nature reserve. Eventually Lange's adoration of nature led him to some extreme views, including the belief that the plants and animals should have the same rights in a garden as the garden owner. Another was the German nurseryman Karl Foerster (1874–1970) who seems to have been the first person specifically to associate ornamental grasses with the natural tendency in gardening.

Foerster assembled plants from around the world and evaluated them in his nursery, offering more than one hundred ornamental grasses for sale as long ago as 1940, a feat few nurseries could emulate even now. Over the years he evolved a naturalistic style of gardening based on his observations of grasses and the plants they grew with in their wild habitats. At the same time, having noticed that, in the wild, grasses provide structure and interest well into winter, when there is little else around, he developed the philosophy of Durchgebluht, meaning bloom throughout (the year). These ideas he extolled in his book *Einzug der Graeser und Farne in die Garten* (Introducing grasses and ferns into the garden), published in 1957, where he wrote of grasses, 'How can these jewels of the garden have been almost completely ignored for so long?' Unfortunately this book has never been translated into English and, since his nursery at Bornim was the wrong side of the Iron Curtain, his ideas had to go a long way round to reach the English-speaking world. His influence in continental Europe, where naturalistic styles of planting have been in vogue for far longer than in the English-speaking world, has been considerable. More important for the English-speaking countries was his influence on a whole generation of nurserymen, gardeners and landscape architects, some of whom worked in his nursery, several then taking his ideas to America in the 1950s. By this time the use of ornamental grasses in continental European gardens was quite common. These émigrés, brimming with Karl Foerster's ideas of naturalistic plantings, were therefore appalled to find they could buy scarcely any grasses in America.

HABITAT AWARENESS

Meanwhile in Europe, Dr Richard Hansen, a disciple of Karl Foerster, working at Weihenstephan near Munich in Germany, researched and developed the idea of using naturalized perennials to form long-lasting, self-sustaining plant communities. These would become so perfectly balanced and so well suited to their garden habitats that there would be no need for the use of expensive and ecologically damaging chemicals, upon which so much traditional Western gardening depended. It is his work that has led to both an increased use of drought-tolerant prairie plants and to the sweeping beds of grasses and forbes (non-grasses) that are a cross between truly wild meadows and traditional borders. His *Die Stauden und ihre Lebensbereuche in Garten und Grunanlagen* (1981) was published in English as *Perennials and their Garden Habitats* (1994). At Westpark in Munich, Rosemarie Weisse has put Hansen's theories into practice, creating flowing, undulating beds of perennials grouped by habitat.

Others influenced by Foerster include the German nurseryman Ernst Pagels, an experienced hybridizer of perennials whose inspired breeding programme has produced the modern hybrid miscanthus; the Belgian landscape architect Jacques Wirtz, who used great swathes of maiden grass (*Miscanthus sinensis* 'Gracillimus') in many of his landscapes and who has created at Schoten in Belgium formal parterres of ornamental grasses; and the Dutchman Piet Oudolf, based at Hummelo in Holland, where he has a nursery and demonstration garden. Oudolf, building on Foerster's ideas, believes that structure is more important than flower, that plants should be set out in seemingly natural combinations, matching habitat with habitat and vigour with vigour, and that colour creates mood. He uses about 20 per cent ornamental grasses in his plantings, the rest being perennials chosen for their ability, like the grasses, to contribute not only flowers but also something to the winter scene, by having interesting seedheads or winter skeletons.

THE AMERICAN MASTERS

It was in America that the ideas advanced by Karl Foerster met up with the Romantic wilderness tradition and the prairie style derived from Jens Jensen, giving rise in due course to the 'new wave' gardens of the Oehme, van Sweden landscape partnership on the East Coast. The philosophy behind the new wave gardens was to bring the prairie into the city and these gardens are in essence stylized prairies, well suited to large urban gardens and public spaces. But it nearly did not happen, for when Wolfgang Oehme arrived in America in the 1950s, eager to put into practice Karl Foerster's ideas, he found that ornamental

Piet Oudolf's naturalistic planting style relies largely on late-season perennials and grasses to create flowing, dynamic masses

composed of plants in which structure is more significant than colour and winter skeletons as important as the flower form.

grasses were still almost unknown there and certainly not available through the normal nursery channels.

Woflgang Oehme, who had studied horticulture and landscape architecture at Berlin University, was much influenced by Karl Foerster's ideas. He moved in the 1950s to Baltimore, where he worked for the Simon family's famous Bluemount Nurseries. There he met Hans Simon who had graduated from Cornell University and subsequently worked for a Swiss nursery, where he not only absorbed Karl Foerster's ideas but also met Kurt Bluemel, another of Karl Foerster's acolytes who, some three years later, joined him at Bluemount. Meanwhile Oehme had persuaded the Simons to grow some ornamental grasses and Bluemount subsequently became the first nursery in America to offer a collection of ornamental grasses.

SMALL BEGINNINGS

Some time later, Bluemel left Bluemount to start his own eponymous nursery. He and Wolfgang Oehme had to beg plants from people's gardens, dig them up from the wild and import seed just to get grasses back into the nursery trade. Even then Bluemel found he had little interest from landscape architects and designers until he started growing the grasses by the thousand: then they saw what could be done with them. At about the same time, Oehme joined forces with James van Sweden to form the Oehme, van Sweden Associates Inc. landscape partnership. Van Sweden had trained as an architect with a particular interest in city planning but, together with Wolfgang Oehme, he developed a style of landscape planting which combined ornamental grasses with typical prairie forbes, the grasses being supplied largely from Bluemel's ever-expanding nursery. Typically, their plantings consist of about 50 per cent largely Asian swaying grasses interspersed with mainly genuine prairie perennials. These were set out in bold, well-defined, interlocking swathes and drifts that have a strong affinity with the plant groupings used by Argentinian Roberto Burle Marx, another of Foerster's disciples. Although these plantings look naturalistic, they are in fact highly stylized and controlled, indeed almost formal, in that each component consists of a single element, whether grass or forbes.

It was around this time that Karl Foerster's ideas were taken to South America by Roberto Burle Marx. In the very different climate of Buenos Aires his naturalistic plantings may look exotic to European and North American eyes, but they are in fact largely composed of plants drawn from his extraordinarily rich native flora. His originality lay in the way in which he massed plants, forming large, often amoeba-shaped blocks, each of a single species, which he then combined in interlocking patterns. It is this use of plants that many modern designers claim has influenced their own planting style.

Thus, while the naturalistic movement has brought ornamental grasses into our gardens, the grasses themselves have changed both how we plant our gardens and what we expect from them.

what is grass?

More plants on earth are grasses than plants of any other kind. The daisy family, the pea family, the orchids and the brambles contain more species, but they are less plentiful in the numbers of individuals. This makes grasses not only the commonest of all plants, but also the most successful. They are the dominant vegetation of open landscapes across the world, from sea level to mountain peaks in every climatic region and in most types of soil. Grasses owe their success to almost endless variations on their essentially simple architecture.

DEFINING TRUE GRASSES

Grasses, in both the narrow and the loose sense, are monocots, belonging to that half of the plant kingdom whose seedlings produce one, not two, seed leaves. Within that branch of the plant kingdom, each group – the true grasses, the sedges, the rushes and the cat-tails – is distinct from the others in readily recognizable ways.

The true grasses constitute the family Poaceae, also known as the Gramineae, a term left over from an earlier system of classification. The family contains some 600 genera and nearly 10,000 species. The majority of them are herbaceous annuals or perennials, though the bamboos, which are also true grasses, are mostly woody.

THE ROOTS

The roots of true grasses are one of the keys to their success. They are fine and fibrous, forming extensive networks that may make up as much as 90 per cent of a grass's dry weight. These roots are capable of penetrating deep into the soil, enabling many species to survive long periods of dryness. Short-grass and mixed-grass prairie grasses, such as buffalo grass (*Buchloe dactyloides*), blue grama (*Bouteloua gracilis*), western wheat grass (*Elymus*) and side-oats grama (*Bouteloua curtipendula*) have roots that may go down 150–200cm, while long-lived tall-grass prairie species such as big blue-stem (*Andropogon gerardii*), Indian grass (*Sorghastrum nutans*), prairie cord grass (*Spartina pectinata*) and switch grass (*Panicum virgatum*) have roots that may extend as much as 7 metres.

Most grasses form an extensive network of roots and root hairs which enable them to survive prolonged periods of dryness.

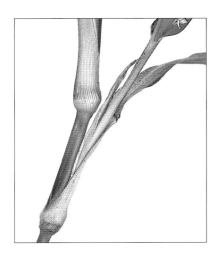

The stems of grasses, known as culms, are composed of solid joints, called nodes, separated by hollow, tubular sections – the internodes. It is these structures which give grasses their great flexible strength.

Sedges can always be identified by the deeply V-shaped section of their leaves (left) as compared to those of grasses (right), which are almost flat. The leaves of woodrushes (*Luzula*) are flat but rolled near the base of the plant (centre).

THE STEMS

Another key factor in the survival of grasses is the flexible strength of their stems, called culms, which are always cylindrical and typically hollow. The cellulose of the walls is reinforced by an oxide of silicon which gives the maturing grass stems their glossy appearance. The silicon serves grasses much as lignin serves trees, enabling them to attain far greater heights than would be possible if they were merely inflated by the pressure of their own sap.

The stems (culms) of grasses are interrupted by joints, called nodes. These are solid partitions which reinforce the tubular strength of the culms at regular intervals, allowing for changes in the direction of the internodal sections – the sections between the nodes, which are always straight. They also form a firm anchor point for the base of each leaf.

THE LEAVES

Grass leaves grow from the base, not the tip as with other plants. This enables them to keep growing when the tip has been removed by grazing or mowing. Each leaf arises from a node, the leaves from alternate nodes being arranged on opposite sides of the culm, forming two ranks. A leaf consists of a split sheath which, originating at a node, is wrapped tightly round the culm, and a blade (commonly referred to as the leaf) which sets off at right angles to the culm. The two are united at the top of the sheath by a ligule (little tongue) which is a small, stiff, shield-like membrane facing the culm. Ligules are almost unique to grasses and, while their function is not fully understood, they may well be there to prevent water and insects, fungi or disease from reaching the soft growing point of the culm concealed within the sheath. The sheath in effect forms a second cylinder

around the culm, reinforcing its tubular strength and forming a double protective barrier around the delicate growing point at the base of each internodal section.

The blades are narrow with parallel veins and usually one prominent vein at the centre, known as the midrib, which is much enlarged and conspicuous, and which adds structural strength to the blade. The upper surface of the blade is covered in stomata which allow the grass to release water vapour into the atmosphere, an essential metabolic process. In many grasses, particularly the prairie grasses, there are groups of larger cells which lose water more quickly than the others. At times, when the roots are unable to take up water fast enough to replace that being lost by these cells, they contract, causing the whole leaf to roll up into a long tube. Since the cells that normally transpire are on the inside of this tube, and the cells on the outside of the tube (the underneath of the leaf) cannot transpire, this action effectively minimizes water loss, enabling these grasses to survive long periods without rain.

THE FLOWERS

The flowers of grasses are their greatest glory and yet, compared with the forbes (non-grasses) that form most of our modern garden flora, the individual flowers of grasses are pretty insignificant, lacking brightly coloured petals, fragrance or even nectar. Considered to be among the most highly evolved of all plants, grass flowers have been reduced to little more than their essential reproductive organs. Each single flower consists of an ovary to which are attached two female organs, the stigmas, and three male organs, the stamens. These reproductive organs are enclosed in two small, bract-like structures: the smaller, inner one is called the palea, the larger, outer one the lemma. The whole assemblage makes up a single floret.

The bract-like structures have no sexual function in themselves, but inflate or deflate to facilitate the reproductive processes. The floret is firstly opened to expose the male organs, allowing them to release their pollen on the wind, after which they are drawn back inside the floret. After a long enough interval to allow the pollen to disperse, the female organs are then exposed in the expectation that they will catch on the wind pollen released by the male organs of a different plant of the same species. Grasses are generally outward breeding, where fertilization can only take place with the pollen of another plant. This is partly achieved by the timing device but also by their unique, highly specialized pollen which contains antigens to prevent self-pollination and facilitate the recognition of suitable pollen. It is these antigens which cause hay fever in susceptible people. The process of releasing or receiving pollen may be repeated more than once a day, for several or many days, a particular species always releasing or receiving pollen at the same times of day.

In most grasses one or more florets are attached to a central axis and enclosed in two larger bract-like structures called glumes. Remarkably, these structures remain constant throughout the grass family, though they vary in size

A typical flower of grass consists of an ovary to which are attached three male organs (the bright yellow pollen sacs in the middle of the picture, right) and two female organs, the spidery stigmas towards the top of the inverted 'V'. The pollen sacs can be a conspicuous feature of many grasses while in flower, as seen in the much magnified spikelet of *Stipa gigantea* shown here.

and shape, the number of reproductive parts and, occasionally, the addition of extra parts. These, together with the lemma, may be associated with hairs or bristles, and may end in a particularly long, sometimes very showy, bristle known as an awn. It is these structures (the florets with their enclosing glumes), rather than the flowers themselves, which give the flowerheads of grasses their amazing luminosity.

FLOWER PANICLES

The spikelets are gathered together into larger flowerheads called panicles, though in many grasses these are not strictly paniculate. The flowerheads of most grasses have a plainly visible central axis called a rachis, and the spikelets can be arranged around this rachis in three basic ways. The simplest is a spike in which the individual spikelets are attached directly to the rachis without intervening stalks. Wheat (*Avena sativa*) and bottlebrush grass (*Hystrix patula*) are examples of this type, which is uncommon.

A raceme (see page 22) differs in having the individual spikelets attached to the central rachis by short stalks, but this is even rarer. The commonest type of flowerhead is indeed the panicle, in which the individual spikelets are attached to the tips of stalks that branch from the rachis. The panicles may be open or closed, open panicles having branches almost at right angles to the rachis and giving a diffuse appearance, as with purple love grass (*Eragrostis spectabilis*), while in closed panicles the branches are upright or almost parallel with the rachis, as in feather reed grass (*Calamagrostis* x *acutiflora*). In most grasses the panicle occurs at the top of the flowering culm, the florets usually containing both male and female organs, but there are exceptions. The pampas grass (*Cortaderia selloana*) has male and female flowers borne on different plants, while with maize (*Zea mays*), the male and female flowers are borne on different parts of the plant, in this case the male flowers at the top of the plant and female flowers at waist level. In wild rice (*Zizania aquatica*), male and female flowers are borne on different parts of the same panicle. The flowers of *Panicum clandestinum* are

cleistogamous, which means that the pollen is transferred from the anther to the stigma without the flower ever opening.

Matters are not always simple, however, and many grasses have flowers that do not fit neatly into these types but are combinations of one or more types, known as compound inflorescences. Moreover, the panicle may not look the same at all stages of its development. For example, in one feather reed grass, *Calamagrostis* x *acutiflora* 'Karl Foerster', the panicle is at first tightly folded up against the rachis, having hardly any width at all. It then fluffs itself out to flower, the branches of the panicle at this stage being fairly widely

Maize (*Zea mays*) is unusual for a grass in presenting its male flowers at the top of the plant and its female flowers at the sides of the stem.

Awns are needle-like or feathery bristles attached to the processes surrounding the ovary in many grasses. It is these, rather than the flowers themselves, that give the flowers of many grasses their amazing ability to catch and hold the light. Shown here are *Hordeum jubatum* (top) and *Hystrix patula* (left), both annual grasses.

spread. Having flowered, the panicle then closes up against the rachis even more tightly than before. The panicle changes colour during this progress, being at first greenish white, then pinky purple as it flowers, finally turning rich, rusty red once flowering is over.

SEEDS

If a flower of grass is successfully pollinated, the ovule inside the ovary turns into a seed or grain, technically a caryopsis, and these can vary greatly in both size and structure. They can be tiny (1–2mm long) as in *Phleum* and *Agrostis*, or much larger, up to 20mm, as in *Avena*, and may be angular, circular or flattened. They may also be flat on one side and rounded on the other, or they may be longitudinally grooved or channelled. Seeds may be hard as flint, as with *Glyceria*, or relatively soft.

More obviously, seed may be naked, as with wheat and rye, many tropical grasses and some ornamental grass genera such as *Sporobolus* and *Eragrostis*, or enclosed in husks. The husks are in fact the remains of the floret, usually consisting of the lemma and palea which may be papery or leathery, or embrace the grain like a skin. Many completely enclose the grain and often adhere to it so closely that they cannot be removed without damaging the grain. The lemmas and palea of many grasses bear barbs, bristles, hairs, teeth or awns which aid in their dispersal, especially if they adhere to passing animals. The awns of many grasses, as in *Stipa barbata*, are twisted when dry, but if soaked in water will unwind themselves, and are often large, as with *Stipa barbata* 'Ecu d'Argent', whose awns can measure 22cm in length, and may be feathery or simply needle-like, as with *Stipa capillaris* or *Hordeum jubatum*.

The seeds of many grasses are enclosed by husks (left) which may bear barbs, bristles, hairs, teeth or awns to aid in their dispersal, especially if the seeds become attached to animals.

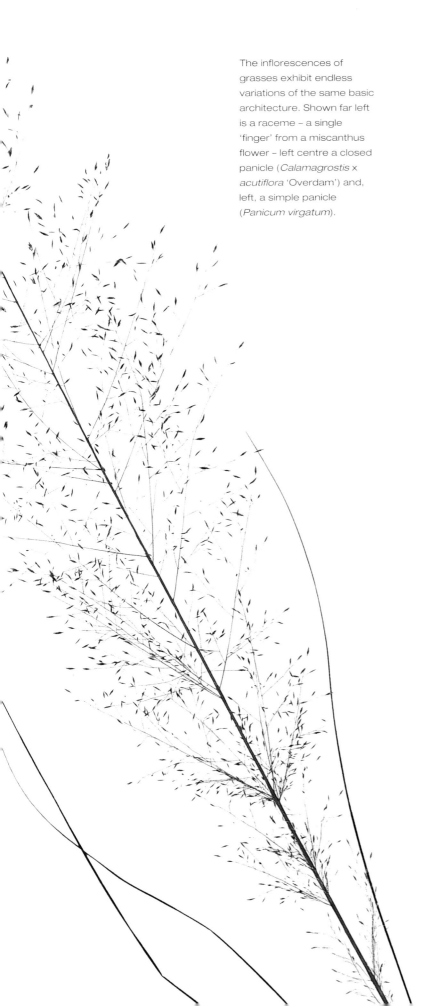

The inflorescences of grasses exhibit endless variations of the same basic architecture. Shown far left is a raceme – a single 'finger' from a miscanthus flower – left centre a closed panicle (*Calamagrostis* x *acutiflora* 'Overdam') and, left, a simple panicle (*Panicum virgatum*).

THE GROWING PLANT

The grass plant itself is just as remarkable as its parts. Most flowering plants have their growing point, or meristem, at the tips of their stems or branches, with the disadvantage that if the meristem is destroyed that part of the plant can make no further growth. Grasses, by contrast, have meristems in two places: one at the base of the leaf, and one just above the node on the culm, so that if the tips of the leaves or stems are damaged or destroyed they can continue to grow. Moreover, the nodal meristems are capable of making more growth on one side of the stem than the other, thus enabling the culm to straighten out if it has been accidentally flattened or trampled.

Grass plants increase in size by the production of lateral shoots at ground level which, in most grasses, then grow on upwards to form new flowering culms. These shoots, called innovations, are produced in the axils of the lowest leaves, usually at ground level. The innovations of tightly clump-forming grasses such as tufted hair grass (*Deschampsia cespitosa*) are formed inside the enveloping basal leaf sheath, bursting out of it as they increase in size – these are called intravaginal innovations. Those of loosely clumping or running grasses such as *Holcus lanata* grow through the sides of the basal sheath and are called extravaginal innovations. This type grow not upwards but outwards, forming underground stems (rhizomes) or above-ground stems (stolons) which can produce new shoots at their nodes. The new shoots then put down roots, not only increasing the size of the colony but in time becoming capable of independent life. *Glyceria maxima* is one example of a grass which spreads by underground rhizomes, while the common reed (*Phragmites communis*) spreads by stolons, above-ground stems that root at their nodes.

A few grasses increase by vivipary, the process by which the flowers are replaced by tiny plantlets. This is genetically fixed in the case of *Deschampsia cespitosa* 'Fairy's Joke' and of *Festuca ovina* 'Vivipara', but it does also occasionally occur in grasses that are under stress, such as that caused by prematurely cold weather in autumn.

SEDGES

The sedges, like the grasses, are a relatively large family, with some 115 genera and about 3,500 species spread across the world but mostly concentrated in wet or damp soils in the temperate and subarctic regions. Most sedges are perennial, with fibrous roots and either rhizomes or stolons, and almost all are evergreen or nearly evergreen. As a group, sedges lack the economic importance of grasses, though a few have their uses.

Separated from the true grasses by aeons of evolutionary time, the sedges can readily be distinguished from grasses by their trimerous nature – that is, all their parts are arranged in threes. The stems are triangular in section, and are solid and without nodes (joints), whereas those of the true grasses are always cylindrical and hollow. Their leaves are also triangular in section, a feature that can easily be felt between thumb and fingers, while the leaves of grasses are always flat. Sedge leaves generally lack ligules (see page 17), or if they are present are greatly reduced: the leaves of grasses always have ligules. The leaf sheaths of sedges are closed – that is, they completely surround the stems and are difficult to pull away: those of the grasses are split and are easy to pull away.

Like the grasses, the sedges are wind-pollinated, but the arrangement of the flowers is quite different. The small individual flowers are usually, but not always, arranged in spikelets. Lacking recognizable petals or sepals, they are not showy, though when gathered into a flowerhead they may have a quiet charm. The spikelets are arranged either in umbels, as in the umbrella plants (*Cyperus*), in spikes, as with *Carex*, or are head-like (with a swollen lump at the tip of the stem), as in *Schoenus*.

The flowers of most sedges are bisexual but in many, including those of the large genus *Carex*, male and female flowers are borne on separate spikes towards the tip of a single flowering stem. The male flower typically has three pollen-producing organs, while the female has three stigma. In the genus *Carex* the female flowers are usually enclosed in an outer structure called a utricle. In a few species the utricle is enlarged, as with *C. grayi*, or brightly coloured, as with *C. baccans*, adding to the flower's ornamental value. In some other *Carex* species the contrast in colouring between male and female flowers can be highly decorative, as with the greater pond sedge (*C. riparia*), where the male flowers at the tip of the stem are black and the female flowers below almost white at the time of exerting their stigmas. Sedge flowerheads are often surrounded by bracts and, although these are often scarcely noticeable, it is these that make the genus *Cyperus*, the umbrella plants, so distinct. In the white-top sedge (*Rhynchospora* species), the bracts are enlarged and appear to be painted white.

The leaves of sedges are often their most ornamental characteristic, those of *Carex* being produced not only in a variety of shades of green but also in yellows, blues, browns and near-reds.

The flowers of rushes have the full complement of floral parts, including petals and sepals, though these are so small that it is difficult to recognize them as such.

The flowerheads of sedges, like the *Cyperus* shown below, are often surrounded by conspicuous bracts, giving rise to their popular name, umbrella plant.

The cigar-like female flowers of cat-tails are much longer lasting than the fleeting male flowers held above them.

RUSHES

The rushes, found worldwide in damp or wet habitats in the cool temperate and and subarctic regions, are a surprisingly small family, with a mere ten genera and no more than 325 species. Rushes have hairy roots with upright or spreading rhizomes, and the leaves are mostly basal, always with sheathing bases but occasionally reduced to the sheaths alone. The leaves may be flat, as in *Luzula*, or rolled (cylindrical) as in *Juncus*. Though wind-pollinated, the flowers have the full complement of floral parts including both petals and sepals, though these are in miniature, arranged in two distinct whorls. They generally have an ovary to which are attached six stamens and three stigma, though some species have male and female flowers on different plants. The tiny flowers, which are greenish or brownish, are gathered together, often in flat-headed cymes but sometimes in panicles, though never showy; one would not grow a rush for its flowers.

Only two genera – *Juncus*, the true rushes, and *Luzula*, the woodrushes – are much grown in gardens and they are much less decorative than true grasses or sedges. The rushes, which generally flower in summer, are natives of wet, sunny habitats, while the woodrushes come from shaded habitats, wet or dry, and can endure considerable summer dryness under deciduous trees.

CAT-TAILS

Cat-tails and reedmaces, though a small family of a single genus, *Typha*, with no more than a dozen or so species, are found across the temperate and tropical world in shallow, freshwater habitats. They spread aggressively by rhizomes and typically colonize large areas in ponds, marshes and at the edges of rivers and lakes, to the exclusion of other plants. Perennial plants, they have stout rhizomes and upright stems, the leaves arranged in two ranks embracing the flowering stem. The thick, spongy leaves, erect at first, arch outwards towards the tip; they are grey-green, turning bright yellow in autumn. They bloom in summer or autumn and are quite different from those of any other grass-like plant.

Both male and female flowers – technically cylindrical, spike-like racemes – are borne at the tops of thick, strong stems around which they are densely clustered. The short-lived male flowers, borne at the tips of the shoots, consist of numerous thread-like filaments which turn golden yellow as the anthers shed their pollen. After flowering, the male flowerhead quickly withers, leaving the tip of the stem bare. The female flowerhead, which is the more conspicuous and longer-lasting, resembles a stout cigar firmly impaled on the stem. It consists of numerous female flowers densely packed together between stiff bristles and is green at first, changing through tan to rich or dark brown as the seeds ripen, often remaining intact well into or through at least part of the winter. In due course the female inflorescence bursts open, looking as though it had been over-stuffed with kapok, releasing on the wind a myriad of tiny nutlets borne aloft on white hairs.

The purpose of design in gardens is to enable the gardener to achieve, by intent, effects that might otherwise come about only by chance, or not at all. Grasses, because their impact is that of structure and line rather than of colour and flower detail, may need to be used somewhat differently from other plants. In the following pages we look at the major underlying principles governing the successful use of grasses in the garden.

Squirrel-tail barley (*Hordeum jubatum*) is one of the few grasses to contribute colour as well as line, though it is the constant reiteration of line, both of leaf and flower, that set the grasses apart from other elements in this beautiful naturalistic planting.

the quality of line

One of the prime qualities of grasses is linearity: the constant reiteration of the curve of leaves and culms cumulatively create an almost unique texture. When using grasses you need always to keep this texture in mind and be aware of how it will harmonize or contrast with other plants and with statuary, pots and buildings.

This texture arises from the repetition of so many almost parallel linear leaf blades. The angles of the lines drawn by the leaves vary greatly, not only from genus to genus and between species, but also from cultivar to cultivar. Among the eulalia grasses, *Miscanthus sinensis* 'Kleine Silberspinne' is notable for the way the exceptionally narrow leaves stand out at right angles to the main stem, making them effectively horizontal, while those of *M. sinensis* 'Gracillimus' or 'Etincelle' arch boldly and gracefully. Similarly, the leaves of *Panicum virgatum* 'Northwind' stand obliquely upright from the stems, unlike those of *P. virgatum* 'Shenandoah' which arch gently away and downward. The leaves may even be pendulous, as in some forms of *Miscanthus* x *giganteus*.

Because the texture of grasses is distinct from that of other plants, and because grasses exert their presence for so much longer than most perennials – often from the time their foliage emerges in spring until decimated by the attrition of winter – they make the ideal framework within which other perennials can flower and fade. In a free-flowing planting in the modern style, grasses can serve, in a naturalistic way, much the same function as yew hedges in the beds and borders of more traditional gardens. Generally, grasses are most effective grown among broad-leaved flowering plants and, to my mind, least effective when grown with other grasses, or among a surfeit of plants with similarly long, narrow leaves.

If you wish to grow grasses with grasses, the best strategy is to contrast extremes. For example, counterpoint the narrow leaves of *Miscanthus sinensis* 'Gracillimus' with the broad, bold leaves of the provencal reed (*Arundo donax*), or the wide, short leaves of deer grass (*Panicum clandestinum*) as a foil to the needle-thin leaves of wavy hair grass (*Deschampsia flexuosa*). Place the ramrod-erect culms of *Calamagrostis* x *acutiflora* 'Karl Foerster' next to fountain grass (*Pennisetum alopecuroides*), with its low mounds of widely arching leaves. Try the solid majesty of *Miscanthus* x *giganteus* with the insubstantiality of a group of switch grass (*Panicum virgatum*). The classic grouping, both for foliage and flower, is *Pennisetum alopecuroides, Panicum virgatum* and *Miscanthus sinensis* against a backdrop of *Arundo donax*.

The obvious contrasts are often the most effective, especially in larger plantings to be read from a distance. These can be created by

The repetition of the flowers and flower stems of many grasses, like *Pennisetum macrourum* shown below, can create a strongly linear effect that few other plants are able to match. Grasses are therefore often best displayed in the garden in situations where this linearity is offset against the solidity of built features, sculpture, containers or plants with broad or rounded foliage, such as bergenias.

The reiteration of the curving linear leaves of grasses creates a unique effect in landscape and garden (above). This can be used either as a background among which plants of contrasting character – either of leaf or flower – may be grown, or as a feature in itself, against a background of broader-leaved plants.

larger plantings to be read from a distance. These can be created by setting the fine foliage of, for example, fountain grasses (*Pennisetum*) against the almost round leaves of bergenias or the large, oval and always erect leaves of the prairie dock (*Silphium*). More subtle effects can be achieved by choosing less obvious partnerships – the relatively broad leaves of wood oats (*Chasmanthium latifolium*) with ferns of the woodland edge, such as lady fern (*Athyrium filix-femina*) or, in a sunnier habitat, bottlebrush grass (*Hystrix patula*) with sun-tolerant male ferns (*Dryopteris filix-mas*). And something approaching harmony can be created by blending *Pennisetum orientale* with tickseed (*Coreopsis verticillata*).

Many grasses have a looseness of form that curves the lines of the leaves and culms, and this can be used to create other contrasts, for example by placing the arching culms of tall *Molinia caerulea* subsp. *arundinacea* 'Zuneigung' or 'Windsaule' against the vertical of an Irish yew or a pencil cedar, or where it can be seen against the clear vertical of the corner of a building. Or contrast the arching mounds of fountain grass foliage (*Pennisetum alopecuroides*) with the horizontals of prostrate conifers, or the narrow arching leaves of prairie cord grass (*Spartina pectinata*) with the large, deeply cut leaves of *Acanthus mollis*.

The flower panicles of many grasses present a fuzzy outline and so need to be contrasted with flowerheads that are linear or have a strongly defined form. Examples include the slender spikes of *Digitalis ferruginea* or *Epilobium*, the looser spikes of *Lythrum*, the twirling spires of *Veronicastrum*, the floating horizontals of *Achillea*, the whorls of *Phlomis russelliana* on their stiff upright stems, the inverted pyramids of the umbellifers and the globe-shaped heads of *Echinops* and *Allium giganteum*. Because they are little more than lines without thickness, the culms and often the panicles of many grasses present no visual barrier: you can see through them to the plants or landscape beyond.

working with light

The design of gardens has much to do with the manipulation of light and it is particularly important when planting ornamental grasses to be aware of how and where the light falls through the day and through the seasons. It is the ability of their flowers and seedheads to catch and hold the light from the sky that gives grasses their unique and very special beauty, making them usually the most luminous plants in the garden. This quality can be used to greatest effect by

The flowers of most grasses are seen to advantage set against a dark background with the sun beyond or beside them, as here, where *Hordeum jubatum* and *Sesleria nitida* positively come alive (below). With the sun behind, the effect would have been quite different and far less visually stimulating.

Sunlight in autumn is far less harsh than that of high summer, tinged with mellow amber tones that mix well with the straw colours of most grasses at this season, as seen here with *Miscanthus sinensis* 'Ghana' and *Stipa gigantea* (right).

planting grasses with the sun beyond or beside them, preferably against a dark background such as the malachite of distant pines or the sombre shadows cast by tall trees.

Other effects are determined by the tonal value of the light which changes through each day and through the seasons. Daylight is whitest and harshest at noon, tinted at dawn with soft pastel pinks and mauves, and most intensely coloured at dusk when the light strikes the earth's atmosphere obliquely, becoming diffused, casting soft shadows and taking on crepuscular tones of yellow, red and orange. Spring light is clear but gentle, in keeping with the dominant yellows, blues and violets of the season, and leaves are yellow rather than green. The light of high summer is harsh and tends to kill colours, so plantings are best designed to be seen early and late, when the light is warmer and the richest colours are revealed. Autumn light is mellow, perfect for the amber waves of fading grasses and their silvery seedheads, best lit from behind by the effulgence of the sun's last rays. The wan light of winter is thin and watery, revealing least colour, just the sere browns and beiges and the green of lawns, all brought vividly to life when rimed with frost.

To make the most of these seasonal changes, it is worth considering associating grasses with perennials and foliage in keeping with the colours of the seasons. In spring, for example, the foliage of grasses is more to the fore than their flowers, so one might use the yellow leaves of Bowles' golden grass (*Milium effusum* 'Aureum'), striped sweet manna grass (*Glyceria maxima* var. *variegata*), and striped ribbon grass (*Phalaris arundinacea* var. *picta* 'Picta') with the blues of bluebells and *Omphalodes cappadocica*, as well as the mauve of *Geranium malviflorum*.

31

using colour

The role of colour in a garden is to create mood. Pale colours such as pinks, blues, mauves, whites and pale yellows are known to be cool and relaxing, while reds, oranges, bright yellows and strong blues are famously hot colours – stimulating and restless. A third option is the baroque, a mood of opulence achieved with deep reds, clarets, terracotta, bronze, lime green and deep purple. By and large, these moods are created not by the grasses but by the plants among which they grow.

Apart from those with coloured foliage, grasses offer little in the way of conspicuous flower colour; rather, they are grown for their structure, their texture and the delicacy of their panicles. They are a counterpoint to the melodies in colour created by other plants. Most grasses are light and airy, producing a relaxed, even calming effect and the insubstantiality of their culms and panicles allows colours created by other plants to drift through them uninterrupted.

The flowers of grasses are subdued in colour, mainly greens and browns, buffs and beige, with a hint of pink or mauve, all neutral tones which can be used as a sorbet between courses of stronger colours or as a sub-plot, weaving their way through a bed or border. Their seedheads mature to richer tones of bronze and gold, ripe corn or straw, just sharp enough to ginger up the colours of any mood. On their own they blend well with the rusty colours of achilleas such as *Achillea* 'Walther Funcke' and *A.* 'Terracotta', with the coppers of heleniums such as *Helenium* 'Moerheim Beauty', and they harmonize with the pinks of astilbes

In modern gardens grasses are used to create structure. Colour, which governs mood, is generally introduced by other plants, mainly perennials. The mood here, with mauves, pinks and silvers, and the dark stems of angelica in the foreground, is calm and gentle.

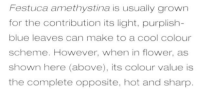

Festuca amethystina is usually grown for the contribution its light, purplish-blue leaves can make to a cool colour scheme. However, when in flower, as shown here (above), its colour value is the complete opposite, hot and sharp.

The structure of this grass (above right) and its ability to catch the light from the sky and draw it down into its flowerheads is more important than the pinky-mauve overtones of its panicles when briefly in flower. The soft, flowing quality of *Calamagrostis brachytricha* is emphasized by the stiffer stance of the plants nearby, especially the red penstemon, which brings positive colour to the planting .

like *Astilbe* 'Amethyst', the mauves of nepetas such as *Nepeta racemosa* 'Walker's Low' or asters such as *Aster* x *frikartii* 'Mönch'.

Grasses with coloured leaves can of course make a major contribution to a given colour theme – reds with reds, blues with blue and so on – and most will contribute for far longer than plants that merely flower. Cool, restful blues abound among grasses, many having leaves, culms and panicles all the same colour. Among them are the more southerly forms of switch grass (*Panicum virgatum*) such as 'Dallas Blues', 'Prairie Sky', 'Heavy Metal' and the tall 'Blue Tower'; blue oat grass (*Helictotrichon sempervirens*), big blue-stem (*Andropogon gerardii*), little blue-stem (*Schizachyrium scoparium*), Indian grass (*Sorghastrum nutans* 'Sioux Blue') and a wealth of small blue fescues. Carnation grasses (*Carex panicea* and *C. flacca*) have blue leaves and will serve in damper, shadier places.

For hot colours, few plants can beat Japanese blood grass (*Imperata cylindrica* 'Rubra'), not only for the intensity of its redness when seen with sun shining through its leaves, but also for the duration of the colour it contributes. Almost as good is the switch grass, *Panicum virgatum* 'Shenandoah'. Few strong yellows compete with the vibrancy of golden Hakone grass (*Hakonechloa macra* 'Aureola' and *H. macra* 'Alboaurea') or the winter colouring of *Luzula sylvatica* 'Aurea'. Taller golds include *Miscanthus* x *giganteus* 'Gotemba' and *M. sinensis* 'Goldfeder'. Yellow is the dominant colour in many grass panicles, especially once they fade and the seedheads ripen to shades of amber, straw and gold. Many New Zealand sedges have leaves in shades of bronze, copper or a verdigris yellow, while red snow grass (*Chionochloa rubra*), a true grass, is at its foxy-red best in winter. All are ideal for a sumptuous baroque-style garden.

massing & grouping

A field of hay ripening under the summer sun, rippled by the wind into amber waves, is generally thought a far finer sight than a single tuft of grass. The same principle applies to ornamental grasses which, when massed or grouped, seem to take on a beauty far beyond the sum of the grasses involved. The best grasses for grouping or massing are those which, when planted together, will blend into a seamless whole. Least successful are those which grow into distinct tufts or mounds, such as the little blue fescues (*Festuca glauca* and its forms) or blue oat grass (*Helictotrichon sempervirens*). These will never run together but will stubbornly persist in retaining their own strongly individual identities. The same is true to a lesser extent of the pampas grasses (*Cortaderia*), especially the New Zealand pampas grass (*C. richardii*).

Although large-scale massing is something few of us can aspire to, the point remains that it is generally more effective to grow grasses in groups than on their own, except when they are used as specimens. Their linearity and uniqueness of texture is most apparent in repetition, and this can be done on a small scale too. Three or four pheasant grasses (*Anemanthele*

Massed plantings of grasses are the hallmark of the New Wave gardens of the Wolfgang Oehme and James van Sweden design partnership. In this garden (below) the massed fountain grasses (*Pennisetum*) are interrupted by occasional clumps of eulalia grass (*Miscanthus*). Such plantings not only appear naturalistic but also form virtually self-maintaining, ecologically sound communities that need little upkeep once established.

lessoniana) grown in a group will reveal their flimsy, flowing character far better than a single grass, especially if that single grass is crammed in between other plants. Similarly, a row of feather reed grass (*Calamagrostis* x *acutiflora* 'Karl Foerster') will appear more densely upright than will a single plant, though here the spacing may be critical. While, as a rule of thumb, grasses should be spaced apart half their height when in flower, slightly closer spacing may be needed when they are massed together. For some grasses, even this is not close enough. Feather reed grasses may look best planted 60cm apart, though the plants will run together sooner if planted only 30cm apart – though half their height in flower would in fact be 75cm. The recommended spacings are given under the individual entries in the Gallery of Grasses (pages 54–135).

Many low-growing grasses make excellent sweeps of ground cover, and this is often an effective way of massing them in smallish gardens. Grasses to use in this way include pheasant grasses, the tufted hair grasses (*Deschampsia cespitosa*), Hakone grass (*Hakonechloa macra*) in its green or yellow forms, prairie dropseed (*Sporobolus heterolepis*), Japanese blood grass (*Imperata cylindrica* 'Rubra'), the smaller – or indeed the taller – eulalia grasses (*Miscanthus*), as well as many sedges (*Carex*) and woodrushes (*Luzula*).

Minimalism is the concept that less is more. By abandoning diversity and complexity it is possible to focus the mind on a single species or variety so that it reveals its very essence. In this garden in Surrey, England, designed by Christopher Bradley-Hole, the forecourt is dominated by a large rectangle planted with a seemingly solid mass of *Calamagrostis* x *acutiflora* 'Karl Foerster' (below).

accents & markers

The modern perception of an accent or specimen is a grass or any other plant which is used deliberately to draw the eye. In Victorian England a specimen was, more specifically, a single special plant, such as a pampas grass, grown in its own in isolation in a hole in the middle of a lawn. The choice of accent plant today is very often a tall grass planted on its own, for any grass – or indeed any other plant – which stands up vertically, to eye level or above, will draw the eye more strongly than a lower-growing plant, especially if it stands above its neighbours. Many grasses can fill this role: the taller eulalia grasses, the provencal reed, many tall moor grasses, the taller prairie switch grasses, such as *Panicum virgatum* 'Blue Tower', 'Cloud Nine' or 'Dallas Blue', and the pampas grasses.

Grasses can draw the eye just as well by virtue of their colouring. Those with white-striped leaves, such as *Miscanthus sinensis* 'Variegatus', *M. sinensis* subsp. *condensatus* 'Cosmopolitan' or 'Cabaret', or the commoner striped ribbon grass, command attention because of their brightness. Less dramatic – and drama is not always a virtue in a garden – are the zebra grasses, such as *Miscanthus sinensis* 'Zebrinus' or 'Strictus', with their leaves transversely banded in cream or yellow.

Grasses do not necessarily have to be large to attract attention. A single clump of a white- or yellow-variegatd grass set among grasses or other plants of similar size with green leaves will draw the eye almost as strongly as a taller plant

Pampas grass (*Cortaderia selloana*) is one of the finest grasses for use as a specimen, its clean, bright white plumes drawing the eye strongly. It is also one of the best of many grasses that continue to look good well into winter, especially when its foliage is dusted with frost

Any grass that has the power to draw the eye may be used as a specimen or marker, whether on account of its colouring or its structure. The foliage of *Elymus hispidus* commands attention because it is so completely different from the colours around it.

– *Calamagrostis* x *acutiflora* 'Overdam' amid a drift of green-leaved feather reed grass, for example, or a golden Hakone grass (*Hakonechloa macra* 'Aureola') among a drift of green-leaved Hakone grasses. or a single blue clump of *Elymus hispidus* or *Sorghastrum nutans* 'Sioux Blue' set in a sea of green foliage.

There are more subtle ways of creating a focus. Grasses with distinct flower or foliage form, such as *Calamagrostis brachytricha*, with its elongated ovoid panicles, or *C. emodensis*, with its uniquely weeping panicles, will draw the eye in a quiet way. So will a single tall moor grass (*Molinia caerulea* subsp. *arundinacea* 'Windspiel'), conspicuous both on account of its fountain-like presence and the way it moves in the wind like dancer, or clumps of the maiden grass (*Miscanthus sinensis* 'Gracilimus' or 'Saraband'), for the distinct texture created by theconstant repetition of their remarkably narrow, slightly curved leaves.

A single specimen may be used to lead the eye to a particular part of the garden, a special feature or an unusual planting scheme, or indeed to distract attention away from something unsightly. An alternative approach is to use a sequence of specimens as markers, definingthe rhythm or spatial pattern of a bed or border. If specimen grasses are repeated in a strictly spaced sequence along a border, they will impel the eye, and hence the feet, along their length. They will still do this if used at the back of a border, but will compel the eye less strongly if their spacing is only approximately equal, bringing a rhythm to the border instead. Golden oat grass (*Stipa gigantea*) is an excellent grass to repeat at the back of a border, the low-growing *Hakonechloa macra* 'Aureola' at the front, or *Miscanthus sinensis* 'Morning Light' somewhere in the middle.

through the year

Planning the successful use of grasses through the seasons depends as much on the choice of companion plants as on the grasses themselves, though the grasses are the main consideration, since they have a longer season of beauty than almost any other kind of plant. The best plantings of ornamental grasses, in both aesthetic and practical terms, are those in which the grasses and their associates share the same garden requirements (moisture lovers with moisture lovers and so on) and are well matched, vigour for vigour. Competition between these plants, once established, will use up the available soil moisture and nutrients, giving weed seedlings little chance.

Since grasses are grown more for their structure than their colour, their best companions are other plants which are strong on structure, especially those which hold their form well into winter. The classic flowerhead shapes to contrast with the airy panicles of grasses and the linearity of their leaves are: (1) the flat heads found on plants such as yarrow and sedums, umbellifers like *Chaerophyllum hirsutum* 'Roseum' and *Anthriscus sylvestris*; (2) spires like those of *Digitalis ferruginea* or *Veronicastrum virginicum*; (3) ball-like or pincushion flowers such as those of *Echinops* and *Knautia macedonica*; (4) loosely structured heads like those of *Astilbe* or goldenrod; and (5) the daisy flowers found on *Rudbeckia*, *Helenium* and *Echinacea*. Give preference to varieties that look good for longest.

WINTER

Grasses, on the whole, go gracefully into winter, often in the full glory of their seedheads, but they look even better if their ethereal panicles can be contrasted with more substantial seedheads. Among the longest lasting are pampas grass (*Cortaderia*), with its massive plumes, the refined eulalia grasses (*Miscanthus*), the tiny grey spikelets of prairie dropseed (*Sporobolus heterolepis*), the dark cloud-like spikelets of switch grass (*Panicum virgatum*), the elegant wands of tall moor grass (*Molinia*), the ovoid heads of Korean feather reed grass (*Calamagrostis brachytricha*) and bristly bottlebrush heads of fountain grass (*Pennisetum*). All can be transformed overnight into fugitive sculptures when rimed by frost or sprinkled with snow, though in milder climates this seldom happens, and their beauty lies rather in the way raindrops bedeck the panicles. Wetness on grasses in winter intensifies their faded colours: the tawny straw of pheasant grass (*Anemanthele lessoniana*), the bleached-out *Stipa tenuissima* and the burnished amber of little blue-stem (*Schizachyrium scoparium*). One could make a picture of these differing tones alone, in keeping with the watery light of winter.

EVERGREEN GRASSES

Evergreen grasses should not be overlooked, for such green brings welcome relief from the dominant neutral colours of the season. Among the best of the

evergreen species are *Ampelodesmos mauritanica*, *Stipa gigantea* and *Deschampsia cespitosa*. Several grasses contribute blue rather than green – the small, silver-blue *Cortaderia selloana* 'Patagonia', *Helictotrichon sempervirens, Elymus hispidus* and *E. solandri* – all look lovely with dark purple crocuses. Many rushes and sedges are evergreen, and these are very useful in the winter garden, especially in their variegated forms, while the New Zealand sedges offer whites, blues, yellows and browns. New Zealand hook sedges (*Uncinia* species) come in burnished reddish-browns. Brightest of all is *Luzula sylvatica* 'Aurea', changing from its summer greenery to an almost gaudy yellow in midwinter.

The best perennials for growing with grasses are those that retain a presence in winter – astilbes, whose faded flowers assume mahogany tones, *Coreopsis verticillata* whose thread-like stems are topped with tiny black buttons, the brown stems of *Rudbeckia fulgida* topped with large black cones, the bulk of *Eupatorium purpureum* which turns light brown, the silver-white wispy stems of Russian sage and the flat heads of sedum.

As important as the grasses is the background against which they are seen, and this is crucial in winter. The skeletal silhouettes of grasses work best against a dark background, ideally the lively, shiny malachite leaves of holly, box or yew. The rusty winter leaves of beech and the paler leaves of hornbeam offer less of a contrast and harmonize with the winter colours of the grasses, creating a distinctly different texture.

Because of the transparency of grasses, especially in winter, it is worth planting beyond them plants whose bark is at its best this season, particularly gleaming white birches such as *Betula utilis* var. *jacquemontii* 'Jermyns'. These can be underplanted with dogwoods grown for their colourful stems. If they in turn are underplanted with *Luzula sylvatica* 'Aurea', bright yellow in midwinter, a winter scene can be created every bit as colourful as the garden in summer.

Grasses take on a new dimension when turned into iced sculptures by frost or a scattering of snow, or revivified when their colouring is intensified by winter wet. Even when winter storms and winds have stripped the seeds from their heads, the skeletons still enchant.

As the attrition of winter gradually strips the grasses of their seeds, a supporting cast of winter flowers becomes more important. Among the earliest shrubs to flower are the witch hazels, the gaunt but fragrant *Viburunum* x *bodnantense*, the evergreen *Garrya elliptica* and the architectural *Mahonia* x *media* 'Lionel Fortescue' whose flowers appear from late autumn, like those of the winter cherry.

Among the earliest perennials to flower are the hellebores, which flower in the depths of winter and mix happily with the evergreen foliage of tufted hair grass, many sedges and the mahogany *Uncinia rubra*. Bergenias, valued for their large, rounded leaves, are perfect for anchoring the airy insubstantiality of grasses. Several, including *Bergenia* 'Sunningdale' and 'Abendglut', have leaves that turn apoplectic crimson in winter, enlivening the wan colours of the grasses and contrasting with the prevailing blues and yellows of the season – aconites, crocus and early daffodils – or with the cream leaves of *Carex oshimensis* 'Evergold'. In small gardens the tiny *Bergenia stracheyi* is a gem to use among smaller, lightly built grasses like *Sporobolus heterolepis* or *Deschampsia flexuosa*.

By the end of winter the litter of dead leaves outweighs the beauty of the remaining grasses and it is time to cut these down so that the beds can be weeded and the new shoots given a chance to emerge unimpeded, allowing Ceres to return from the underworld, and the cycle of the season to start over.

SPRING

By the time the warm season grasses are cut down in late winter, the cool season growers are already well furnished with foliage. Among the first into leaf in spring are the lowly striped Yorkshire fog (*Holcus mollis* 'Albovariegatus') and the brighter, white-edged *Arrhenatherum elatius* subsp. *bulbosum* 'Variegatum', followed closely by the tall striped feather reed grass (*Calamagrostis* x *acutiflora* 'Overdam') and striped ribbon grasses (*Phalaris arundinacea*), both of which have leaves tinted pink at first. The first two are ideal for underplanting with spring bulbs but the last two are vigorous and associate better with the colourful new growth of strong-growing perennials such as paeonies, whose leaves are plum-purple at first, or crown imperials, with lime-green leaves. Cream-striped sweet manna grass (*Glyceria maxima* var. *variegata*) prefers to grow in ground too wet for most early bulbs, and is better grown with moisture-loving plants, for example *Primula rosea*, spring snowflake and snake's-head fritillary. In shade, Bowles' golden grass (*Milium effusum* 'Aureum') is one of the earliest grasses to come into leaf, in time for the little blue bulbs of spring – scillas, chionodoxa, pushkinia, grape hyacinths and the true blues of *Corydalis flexuosa*.

GRASSES IN FLOWER

Green moor grass (*Sesleria heufleriana*) is one of the first grasses to come into flower, among the snowdrops and crocuses. Its spikelets are produced in short, dense spikes at the ends of slender stalks; they are almost black, but virtually

hidden for a while by the abundance of showy, creamy-white pollen sacs. Another moor grass to flower this early is the mound-forming *S. nitida* which produces little black flowers at the tips of slender, blue-grey stems. The first of the hair grasses, *Deschampsia wibelliana* starts to flower in mid-spring, earlier than the tufted hair grasses (*D. cespitosa*) which flower a month later. The small blue *Poa colensoi* flowers now but, like the little blue fescues it resembles, the flowers and culms are the same colour as the leaves and tend to go unnoticed.

Many sedges flower early enough in the year not to have to compete with true grasses, so their quiet charm is doubly valuable. Most are particularly useful in shade since they will do much better here than grasses. They mix happily with woodland flowers like snowdrops, wood anemones and the smaller, especially species, daffodils. The showiest of these early sedges is *Carex plantaginea*, whose pleated leaves have a fancied resemblance to those of a plantain. This sedge produces almost black flowerheads made conspicuous by long white anthers for several weeks. Variegated sedges are often most telling in shade. Among the earliest to flower are *Carex* 'Ice Dance', *C. morrowii* (the faintly white-edged 'Variegata', the more vigorous, creamy-yellow striped 'Fisher's Form' or the smaller 'Gilt'), *C. siderosticha* 'Variegata', as well as striped *C. riparia* 'Variegata' whose leaves, pure white at first, make a dramatic contrast with the black flowers. Bowles' golden sedge (*C. elata* 'Aurea') flowers just a little later, as does the much taller blue-leaved San Diego sedge (*C. spissa*).

Most woodrushes flower early, as one would expect of woodland-floor plants. They tolerate even deeper shade than the sedges, and drier conditions. *Luzula nivea* is showier than the common woodrush (*L. sylvatica*) both because of the white hairs that fringe its leaves and its small heads of nearly white flowers. Two woodrushes with coloured foliage are brighter – *L. sylvatica* 'Taggart's Cream' whose new leaves emerge pure white, passing through cream to green, and *L. sylvatica* 'Aurea', whose winter leaves turn garish yellow. These combine happily with *Arum italicum* 'Marmoratum', all three tolerating dry soils and being showy in the same season. They also associate well with New Zealand sedges with coloured leaves such as *C. comans* and *C. comans* bronze, 'Frosted Curls' or 'Taranaki' and the blue-leaved *C. trifida* 'Chatham Blue', as well as the New Zealand hook sedges such as mahogany-brown *Uncinia rubra* or *U. uncinata*.

Grasses underplanted with spring bulbs will provide colour and interest when the grasses have been cut down. The season may start with snowdrops which, with careful selection of species and varieties, may continue to flower until

The very picture of Primavera (left) – a planting of the blues and light yellows so typical of spring. Bowles' golden grass (*Milium effusum* 'Aureum') draws the eye into this ground cover planting of wood anemones, the leaves of the grass being more luminous than the blue of the flowers, which will appear to fade away altogether when seen from a distance.

the daffodils appear. Daffodils are the obvious bulbs with which to underplant grasses and the perennials that go with them. They range in stature from diminutive species for the front of the border, to varieties 60–80cm tall, which may be in flower among the stronger-growing warm season grasses. Since grasses bring to the garden an air of the natural world, the daffodils that go best with them are the wild species with smaller, simpler flowers, especially if they are to be naturalized in meadow-like plantings. The daffodil season overlaps that of the tulips, which bring with them a totally different range of colours. As with daffodils, the tulips that mix most easily with grasses are those with the simplest flower form, the Triumph or mid-season tulips, the Darwin tulips, and the single or cottage tulips. Contrary though it may seem, in small gardens it is the bright reds and yellows among the tulips which look most natural when planted among the grasses: subtle schemes of pinks, mauves, purples look contrived when used in small quantities. Camassias, which have flowers in white or shades of blue, have a season of some two months and are vigorous enough to compete with the increasing leafage on the growing clumps of warm season grasses.

SUMMER

Grasses, to begin with, play a minor role amid the summer splendour of roses, late rhododendrons, pungent magnolias and sweet-scented philadelphus, lilacs, lavenders, the acid gold of alchemilla, astilbes and alstroemeria, aruncus and astrantia, campanulas and cardiocrinums, *Centranthus ruber*, delphiniums and gypsophila, the first hardy geraniums, lilies and daylilies, peonies, penstemons, nepeta and phlomis. They contribute mainly the light relief of their foliage, the restful reiteration of line, the constant curving of their leaves and the sound of wind through them. But as summer draws on, increasing numbers of grasses come into flower so that by late summer or early autumn theirs is often the dominant presence, though much depends on proportion.

Most of those grasses that come into flower at the beginning of summer will continue to contribute to the garden until autumn. Two are in the first rank of ornamental grasses, *Stipa gigantea* and *Calamagrostis* x *acutiflora* 'Karl Foerster'. Golden oats grass, the former, is the most beautiful of these, with its gently swaying culms bearing huge heads of long-awned, golden flowers. The latter is the most striking, with its stiffly upright habit and narrow plumes of sterile, foxy-red flowers. Tufted hair grass (*Deschampsia cespitosa*), which flowers at the same time, is useful since it will grow in sun or shade, damp or dry. While these can be grown as single specimens among delphiniums, peonies and *Campanula lactiflora*, they are even more impressive massed – especially if the plants among which they grow are also massed. These might include early umbellifers such as *Chaerophyllum hirsutum* 'Roseum', thistle-like *Cirsium rivulare* 'Atropurpureum' and *Knautia macedonica* and the first of the prairie daisies *Helenium, Helianthus* and *Ratibida*.

High to late summer reveals the garden at its fullest, dense with foliage and flowers, rich in colour and ripening seedheads. The strength of this planting lies in the dynamic tension between the sculptural solidity of the clipped beech trees and the insubstantiality of the massed groups of grasses, including *Miscanthus sinensis* 'Kleine Silberspinne' and *Calamagrostis* x *acutiflora* 'Karl Foerster'. (The same garden is shown in winter on page 39, in autumn on page 45 and, with a detail of its rill, on page 53.)

Many stipas come into flower in high summer, including the wispy jade-green *Stipa tenuissima* and *S. calamagrostis* with its lax habit and similar flowers. The so-called needle grasses, also stipas (*S. spartea, S. turkestanica, S. capillata*) and the feather grasses (*S. pennata* and *S. barbata*) with long, feathery awns, flower now, as do the melics – not only the woodlanders like *Melica nutans and M. uniflora*, but also the showier *M. altissima* and the smaller *M. transsilvanica*, both beloved of flower arrangers for their sultry maroon-purple flowers, as well as the low-growing *M. macra*, with its chaffy, parchment-white flowers. None has a long season of interest, though they are ravishing enough while in flower.

The little blue fescues flower at this time, though as they are grown mainly for their foliage many gardeners remove their flowers. The annual squirrel-tail grass (*Hordeum jubatum*), when grown on light soils, will flower all summer, though not so freely as at its first flush. *Avena sterilis* flowers now and, ripening to the colour of corn, lasts until the end of the season. These grasses overlap and look lovely with the last of the lily-flowering tulips, the most garden-worthy of the camassias, *Camassia leichtlinii*, with summer bulbs such as *Fritillaria persica* and the spectacular *Allium hollandicum* 'Purple Sensation', many lilies starting with *Lilium candidum* and the dramatic foxtail lilies (*Eremurus*).

The art is to combine grasses not just with the first flush of perennials but also with those that come later, and with those that will go into winter with them, bearing in mind that other combinations may be more suitable for grasses that come into flower later in the summer. One strategy is to use perennials that have exceptionally long flowering seasons, like *Verbena bonariensis* and *Coreopsis verticillata*, both of which bloom from early to late summer. Other long-flowering perennials include *Cirsium rivulare, Knautia macedonica, Scabiosa atropurpurea* 'Chile Black' and *Gaura lindheimeri*, with its pink or white butterfly flowers.

The first warm season grasses come into flower in midsummer, notable among them the white *Pennisetum villosum* and the pinkish *P. orientale* and its forms, all of which mix well with pink, mauve and white flowers, including roses. The earliest of the eulalia grasses are *Miscanthus sinensis* 'Ferner Osten' and *M. sinensis* 'China', which produce flowers of an almost startlingly bright vinous red. Other eulalia grasses follow, though many do not open until autumn.

By the time these grasses are in flower, so are agapanthus, crocosmias and crinums, the hybrid daylilies and the real lilies, as well as the first of the late season perennials – *Rudbeckia, Eupatorium, Acanthus, Achillea millefolium, Liatris, Monarda, Nepeta, Veronica, Veronicastrum, Echinacea, Artemisia ludoviciana, Limonium*, penstemons, phloxes, sedums and late sunflowers, *Solidago* and early asters such as *Aster* x *frikartii* 'Mönch'. These coincide with the last of the annual grasses to flower, the mahogany-red *Pennisetum setaceum* 'Rubrum', the giant *Panicum miliaceum* 'Violaceum' and *Sorghum nigrum*; the latter two both bear heavy heads of dark seeds.

As the seasons change in this Tom Stuart-Smith garden (above), so do the spatial and colour relationships between the different plants, altering the mood of the planting to one of autumn mellowness.

As the fullness of summer passes through the ripeness of autumn, grasses reveal new aspects of their beauty. Where once the flowers of these eulalia grasses (right) shimmered in flamboyant summer colours of vinous reds, pinks and silver, in autumn they take on tones of ripened straw, burnt umber and raw sienna, while their leaves turn to lustrous yellows, ambers and ochres.

AUTUMN

In autumn most of the warm season grasses are at their peak, either abundantly in flower or segueing into silvery seeds. Many assume richly glowing colours: the amber of big blue-stem and *Sporobolus heterolepis*, straw tones of *Miscanthus sinensis* 'Malepartus', rusted iron of little blue-stem, clear yellow of *Panicum virgatum* 'Strictum', the wine red of *P. virgatum* 'Shenandoah' and *Hakonechloa macra*, all looking brighter if contrasted with a few evergreens, including tufted hair grass, golden oats grass and *Ampelodesmos mauritanica*. The flowers of *Chasmanthium latifolium* turn copper-red in autumn and look as though they have been carved from solid mahogany, then polished, while the leaves of the moor grasses (*Molinia*) turn bright butter-yellow. The intensity of autumn colour depends largely on the amount of sun the plants absorbed in summer. Under the blazing summer skies of continental climates the colours are strongest, and more muted under the greyer skies of maritime climates or if grown in shade.

Ideally these grasses should be planted where they can be seen with the sun beyond or beside them, with a darker background behind, and mixed with shrubs and trees that also colour well in autumn. Then, as they turn, the leaves of the grasses will burn with an effulgence similar to that of the trees, their silvery flowers almost sparkling in the light.

The foreground flowers of autumn, all of which blend well with grasses, include red, pink or white *Schizostylis, Nerine*, hardy *Amaryllis* and *Liriope*, with their mauve, purple, pink or even white spikes of muscari-like flowers that last into winter. Sedums, also foreground plants, flower in summer but are grown, in the context of grasses, as much for their autumnal seedheads, which pass through shades of twilight mauves and purples to contrasting blacks and browns.

The flowers of the prairies peak at the same time as the grasses – the copper or yellow daisies of heleniums and *Rudbeckia fulgida* 'Goldsturm', the paler yellows of *Helianthus* 'Lemon Queen', x *Solidaster* 'Super' and *Solidago* 'Goldenmosa' and the late, bright yellow flowers of *Helianthus salicifolius*. These colours lead into the cinnabar reds of other heleniums like *Helenium* 'Moerheim Beauty', the darker 'Rubinkuppel' and the shorter 'Kupferzwerg', colours which seem singularly appropriate to autumn.

The mournful mauves of autumn asters are a perfect foil for the silvery seedheads of eulalia grasses and prairie dropseed, mauves and purples always at their best when combined with greys and silver. The richly coloured *Aster* x *frikartii* 'Mönch' is one of the best, flowering for weeks on end and, being relatively low-growing, it makes an excellent foreground to many of the shorter grasses such as *Miscanthus sinensis* 'Flamingo' or 'Kleine Silberspinne'. Many of these and the grasses that grow with them will bring colour to the garden well into winter.

gardeners' meadows

Meadows are so-called because they are mown (from the Old English *mawan*, to mow). But, unlike lawns, which are mown with great frequency, true meadows are usually mown twice, for silage in early summer and for hay in late summer. In places where the climax vegetation is deciduous forest, mowing prevents woody plants from becoming established, allowing a complex mixture of bulbs and perennials to flourish in a matrix of grasses. While farmers expect their meadows to be dominated by grasses, gardeners expect their meadows to abound with flowers. Indeed, the dream of a flowering meadow – the flowery mead of mediaeval romance – seems to offer the possibility of an abundance of flowers in return for little more than mowing twice a season. In practice, it's not that simple.

Soil fertility is the crux. Meadows occur naturally on poor soils, and most garden soils are too rich, with the result that attempted meadows soon become swamped by invasive mat-forming grasses and rampant weeds. Fertility can be reduced by repeatedly mowing the grass closely and removing the mowings, for a season or more, while the vigour of the grasses can be reduced by introducing the parasitic but pretty yellow rattle (*Rhinanthus minor*). After that, wildflowers may appear spontaneously among the grasses, including dandelion, celandine, buttercups, red clover, hawksbeard, corncockle and ox-eye daisies, to which can later be added bulbs such as crocuses, small daffodils, alliums, muscari, scillas and snake's head fritillaries, all of which should seed themselves once established.

A more radical way to reduce soil fertility is to scrape off the topsoil and work with the less fertile subsoil, having first destroyed deep-rooted perennial weeds such as docks and bindweed. The area can then be sown with a mixture of suitable grasses and wildflowers; many seed merchants make up mixes to suit different soils. If the first method is adopted, wildflowers will appear unbidden once the mowing regime is changed, and over the years more and more will add themselves. As Britain has a rather limited palette of wildflowers compared with continental Europe or America, gardeners often like to enrich their meadows with the wildflowers of other countries. These can be introduced as plugs and might include yarrow, harebell, selfheal, ox-eye daisy, meadow cranesbill and other geraniums, field scabious and greater knapweed from Europe, and butterfly weed, lanceleaf coreopsis, bergamot, smooth aster, smooth penstemon and blue wild indigo from North America.

Gardeners' meadows attempt to create the romantic feel of a wild meadow, with its rich mixture of grasses, flowers, birds, butterflies and bees, without replicating the exact composition of a real meadow. This is necessary largely because gardeners' meadows are made over a relatively short time, on soils that are usually far too rich for genuine meadow grasses and flowers. The meadow below has been created using tufted hair grass together with perennials known to thrive on richer soils, such as foxgloves and wild onions.

Siting is important. A meadow will be most effective sited in sun for at least six hours a day, against a dark background of hedges or evergreens; it should be defined in the foreground by a path or strip of mown grass. Orchard meadows are necessarily in shade, but still need defining so they are not mistaken for somewhere that got forgotten.

The choice of grasses is crucial; coarse, rampant grasses will give wildflowers no chance. Among the best for meadows are sweet vernal grass (*Anthoxanthum odoratum*), always the first to flower, scenting whole meadows with its fragrance, common bent (*Agrostis capillaris*), several fescues including red (*Festuca rubra, F. rubra* subsp. *littoralis*), Chewing's (*F. rubra* subsp. *commutata*), dwarf (*F. valesiaca* subsp. *pseudovina*) and meadow fescue (*F. pratensis*), with meadow foxtail grass (*Alopecurus pratensis*), crested dog's tail (*Cynosurus cristatus*), common quaking grass (*Briza media*), Timothy grass (*Phleum pratense*) and meadow

Meadows occur naturally on soils of low fertility. They are composed of a mix of cool season grasses, bulbs and herbs and are maintained in equilibrium by the simple act of mowing once or twice a year. Mowing prevents woody plants from becoming established, but timing is critical if the various grasses and wildflowers are to seed themselves successfully. The overall effect of a meadow should be pointilliste rather than broad brush, and will change from year to year, partly because seeders like Queen Anne's lace, ox-eye daisy and red poppies may flourish at first, then fade, once the more permanent plants establish themselves.

barley (*Hordeum secalinum*). Larger alien grasses such as *Ampelodesmos mauritanica, Stipa gigantea* or *Calamagrostis brachytricha* can be used in drifts to draw the eye to, or away from, particular parts of the meadow or background.

Shaded meadows grow different flowers and grasses. Self-seeders like foxgloves, cow parsley and rosebay willowherb will dominate in the early years, underplanted with bulbs large and small including daffodils and snake's head fritillaries, while later exotics such as camassias and tulips can be added. Suitable grasses include tufted hair grass (*Deschampsia cespitosa*), wavy hair grass (*D. flexuosa*), purple moor grass (*Molinia caerulea* subsp. *caerulea*), the pale-leaved European woodlander *Brachypodium sylvaticum*, wood brome (*Bromus ramosus*), broad-leaved meadow grass (*Poa chaixii*), and, in light shade, the yellow-green leaved, autumn-flowering *Sesleria autumnalis*, with tufts or drifts of sedges like *Carex muskingumensis* or snowy woodrush (*Luzula pilosa*). Falling fruits will enrich the ground, encouraging coarse grasses, so should be removed.

gardeners' prairies

Prairies, like meadows, are grasslands but whereas meadows are made up of cool season grasses and herbs growing on poor soils and are maintained by mowing, prairies are a climax vegetation, made up mainly of warm season grasses and flowers growing on rich soils. The prairies of North America were shaped by rainfall or the lack of it, by the severity of winter cold and the searing heat of summer, by howling winds which vastly increase evaporation. In other countries, with other soils and different climates, the prairie plants grow differently so that it is impossible to replicate a real prairie. In northern Europe, cool season grasses and perennials take over, swamping the genuine prairie flora before it can establish itself.

The flora of the prairie contains some of the world's finest grasses and showiest flowers. Many have long been used in beds and borders but have not always sat easily with the other, often over-bred denizens of these borders. They fit in more happily with the naturalistic European movement in planting developed through the ideas of William Robinson and Karl Foerster, and the gardens of Mien Ruys and Jens Jensen, the formalized prairies of the Oehme, van Sweden partnership and the stylized prairies of Piet Oudolf.

Like Karl Foerster, Piet Oudolf assembled plants from around the world in search of material from which to create seemingly natural combinations in the garden. From among these, Oudolf selected mainly prairie plants that will grow well in a wide range of soils and will provide a long season of colour and interest.

In damp, equable climates it is almost impossible to replicate genuine prairies, which are the product of aeons of low rainfall and high evaporation, scorching summers, freezing winters and dessicating winds. Instead, colourful prairie-style plantings can be made using a mixture of genuine prairie plants and grasses in conjunction with perennials, grasses and bulbs from other parts of the world. The result is seen here in Mary Payne's naturalistic prairie-style planting in Somerset, England. The plants are allowed some freedom to seed and to find for themselves those conditions which suit them best.

The Prairie Style pioneered by Piet Oudolf draws its inspiration from the naturalistic movement in continental Europe and seeks to combine plants in ways similar to those found in wild plant communities. The resulting gardens, which rely heavily on genuine prairie perennials and grasses, are a cross between an idealized prairie and the traditional herbaceous border – more colourful than a real prairie and more formal than a wild plant community. About 20 per cent of the plants in a typical New Perennial planting by Piet Oudolf will be grasses. This garden (right) is the Millennium Garden at Pensthorpe Nature Reserve and Gardens in Norfolk, England; it had been established for about four years at the time it was photographed.

Just as importantly, Oudolf found new ways to combine these plants, largely based on his observations of wild plant communities. While in genuine prairies the flowers and grasses grow together with individual plants intermingling, in the Prairie Style the species are deliberately segregated – a group of Culver's root, for example, standing next to a group of prairie switch grass, but not mingling with it. The result is that the new Prairie Style looks more organized than a genuine prairie, but still far less the victim of artifice than the borders of Gertrude Jekyll. To the genuine prairie flora are added plants from around the world that also contribute to the general look of naturalism – galega and goat's beard from Europe, astilbes from China, foxgloves from Europe and polygonums from the Himalayas, nepeta from Africa, as well as grasses such as *Miscanthus* from Japan and Korea, feather reed grass (*Calamagrostis* x *acutiflora*) from Europe and fountain grass (*Pennisetum*) from Africa.

In Oudolf's own garden, naturalistic plantings of perennials and grasses are set within the formality of green lawns and neatly clipped yew hedges whose tops undulate in wave-like patterns. In larger gardens and parks, structure is created by the size of the groups of plants, each species or variety being planted in a mass of just that one variety, a further structural element being paths of a contrasting material running right through the planting.

The key to success with these gardens is to clear and prepare the ground thoroughly before planting, and to place plants of similar vigour next to each other so that none overwhelms others. Once established, they can be left for several years with little further work. If there is a downside to the Prairie Style it is that the prairie plants are mostly late flowering, producing their greatest impact from midsummer through until autumn, often continuing to contribute to the garden through the winter, stripped down to their skeletal forms. The season can be extended by adding spring- and early-summer flowering bulbs, but adding early perennials merely waters down the late-season impact.

woodland & shade

Woodland and shade are not the easiest habitats in which to grow ornamental grasses for the simple reason that grasses are primarily plants of open, sunny places. In the wild the true grasses do not grow in deep shade but they will grow at the edge of woodland and in glades or clearings where the sun can penetrate. In deeper woodland it is the sedges and woodrushes that flourish. Bearing this in mind, it is possible to create enchanting effects with grasses in shaded areas.

Among the most reliable grasses for shade are the hair grasses, both tufted (*Deschampsia cespitosa*), found in the wild on wet and badly drained soils, and crinkled (*D. flexuosa*), most at home on dry sandy and peaty soils. In the wild the spaces between clumps of tufted hair grass are often filled by carpets of English bluebells, while crinkled hair grass is often accompanied by wood anemones. The bottlebrush grass (*Hystrix patula*), with its spiky pink and green flowers, is a native of damp woodlands, while wild wood oats (*Chasmanthium latifolium*), with its flattened, mahogany lockets, will tolerate, but not excel in, dry conditions.

Indispensable in large shaded areas are the bromes and false bromes, the jade-green *Bromus aleutensis* and *B. ramosus*, with their 180cm tall culms of pendulous panicles with distinctly bristly spikelets, and *Brachypodiumn sylvaticum* with rather stiffly held, upright, slightly arching panicles and long-awned spikelets. All three are easily grown in woodland or shade and self-seed freely enough to create dense ground cover. The small wood reed or bush grass (*Calamagrostis epigejos*) is not as showy as feather reed grass (*C.* x *acutiflora*), of which it is one parent, but will usefully grow in damp or wet ground and on heavy soils, if the

With a careful choice of species it is possible to make enchanting plantings of ornamental grasses in woodland, as shown in this garden by Wolfgang Oehme and James van Sweden. Drifts of a single species are far more restful than mixed plantings using a great number of different grasses and flowers. The fountain grasses (*Pennisetum*) used here will only succeed in shade in relatively hot summer areas with high light intensity. In cooler climates, under greyer skies, tufted hair grass (*Deschampsia cespitosa*) would be a better choice.

Bowles' golden grass (*Milium effusum* 'Aureum') is one of the finest for woodland and shade where it will seed itself around lightly without ever becoming a problem. It mixes well with many woodland plants, such as the Lenten roses and birch shown here, and associates well with the blues and yellows that predominate in spring. Like many cool season growers, it tends to go dormant or semi-dormant in summer and so is unsuitable for massing.

shade is not too dense. In a quieter idiom are two small melics, *Melica uniflora* and *M. nutans*. Their prime quality is daintiness, both in the poise of their thin leaves and the presentation of their sparse panicles. They provide an ideal foil for small ferns, woodland bulbs and low perennials like violets.

Coloured and variegated grasses can be used to draw the eye. *Milium effusum* 'Aureum' is a soft yellow in shade, perfect with the blues of spring woodland bulbs. *Holcus mollis* 'Albovariegatus' is another grass that grows happily in shade, its tendency to summer dormancy being less pronounced there. The variegated wood melic (*Melica uniflora* 'Variegata') has greyish-white stripes on leaves so thin they seem almost transparent. By comparison the leaf colour of *Hakonechloa macra* 'Aureola' is positively brash, though more subdued in shade than in sun. It can be used to draw the eye or to lead from woodland into more sunlit areas.

Several grasses usually grown in sunnier parts of the garden will grow well at the edge of woodland and in glades, though the effect of shade will be to make them grow more lax and flower less freely. Among these are the eulalia grasses, especially *Miscanthus* 'Purpurascens' and others which colour well in autumn, the switch grasses (*Panicum virgatum*) and the plume grasses (*Saccharum* species).

SEDGES AND WOODRUSHES

While most sedges grow in shade, especially if the soil is damp, it is worth exploiting their diversity to achieve contrasting effects. The broad, flat leaves of *Carex plantaginea* present a rosette and lie flat on the ground, whereas those of *C. phyllocephala* and *C. muskingumensis* are carried in a whorl at the top of an upright stem. Variations in leaf colour can be used to advantage too, the broad blue leaves of *C. flaccosperma*, for example, set beside the dark green of *C. pendula* or the yellow-green of *C. flava* or *C. elata* 'Aurea' which is bright yellow edged with dark green. Of the glaucous-leaved sedges, *C. flaccosperma* is outstanding with its wide leaves, as is *C. spissa* for its narrow, arching blue foliage. New Zealand sedges come in several colours: *C. kaloides* is almost orange, as is *C. testacea*, while *C. flagellifera, C. buchananii, C. petriei* and *C. comans* are differing shades of brown.

Few woodrushes are stars but they provide an excellent foil for many other plants and have, moreover, the virtue of growing in drier situations and in denser shade than any other grass-like plant. They make ideal carpets beneath shrubs or between larger perennials, and diminutive species such as *Luzula luzuloides* and *L. campestris* can be used to create the effect of lawn in woodland openings.

the water's edge

Water is in many ways the perfect foil for ornamental grasses, providing several points and counterpoints of contrast: the broadness of an open sheet of water with the widthless linearity of the grasses, the simplicity of still water with the complexity of their leaf patterns, the supine flatness of water with the slender verticality of grasses, the immobility of still water with the movement of the wind through the grasses, the darkness of deep water with the light-catching qualities of the flowers and seedheads of grasses or their variegated leaves, and their images reflected, and inverted, in the water.

Water extends the range of plants that can be grown as companions to the grasses, adding further contrasts. Consider, with the linearity of grasses, the almost circular pads of water lilies, the arrow-shaped leaves of *Sagittaria* and arum lilies, the long, oval leaves of water hawthorn, golden club, water plantain, or bog arum, as well as the giant paddle-shaped leaves of lysichitons and the heart-shaped leaves of colocasias. But there are affinities, too, that can work in subtler ways. Bog and water irises have sword-shaped leaves, often held rigidly erect, as does *Acorus calamus* and its variegated form, and *Equisetum hyemale* and the transversely banded *E.* 'Bandit', whose stems are always very upright. Such erect leaves and stems can emphasize the arching nature of the foliage of grasses such as *Glyceria maxima, G. maxima* var. *variegata* or *Spartina pectinata* 'Aureomarginata'.

The banks of a natural stream (left) are saturated with water, providing an ideal habitat for many sedges, rushes and cat-tails. Both the camassias in the foreground and the Bowles' golden sedge enjoy these conditions.

Where ponds or streams have a concrete or synthetic liner (below left), the surrounding ground may be as dry as dust and totally unsuitable for moisture-loving plants. But many grasses have a vigour and opulence that create a lush illusion, especially when reflected in still water as in this Chesapeake Bay garden designed by Oehme and van Sweden.

In this contemporary garden by Tom Stuart-Smith (below) the water, with its strongly defined edge, serves an architectural rather than an ecological function. The planting makes little concession to the presence of water, other than as a medium for reflection. Note the contrasting shapes of the two grasses on the right of the water, and how the dark background of trees sets off their lightness of form.

Because all plants need water, the expectation is that those growing in or near water will grow larger and more lushly than other plants. Some certainly do, like the giant *Gunnera manicata*, the yellow, cream and white lysichitons, and the giant ragworts (*Senecio*). Yet problems arise in gardens where the water is separated from dry land by concrete or a liner, for these plants will fail if grown in dry ground, and may need to be planted in containers set within the pond itself. The illusion of giantism can be maintained in dry ground by growing tall grasses, like *Miscanthus sinensis* 'Roland' or 'Silberturm', *M. sinensis* var. *condensatus* 'Cosmo Revert' or the giant provencal reed (*Arundo donax*), along with large-leaved perennials such as the prairie dock or *Bergenia ciliata*.

The sheer size of these waterside plants creates a problem. Vertical forms present themselves strongly to the eye and it is all too easy to plant tall grasses and perennials at the water's edge only to find that they create a barrier to the imagination. Better by far to grade the planting from the water's surface – littered, perhaps, with flat lily pads – through transitional plants such as water soldiers or *Caltha palustris*, which break the surface of the water enough to create a change of texture, to slightly taller marginals such as water iris, *Sagittaria* or pickerel weed, thence to the rounded shape of grasses of moderate growth – *Spartina pectinata* or *Miscanthus sinensis* 'Flamingo' or 'China'. *Gunnera manicata* backed by *Miscanthus sacchariflorus* can follow in turn, if space permits, backed by the even taller provencal reed (*Arundo donax*). In general it is more effective to use bigger clumps or drifts of fewer species than a miscellany of singletons.

gallery of grasses

Several hundred ornamental grasses are readily available today through garden centres, specialist nurseries and by mail order. In the following pages we present portraits of a representative selection of the very best. Other worthwhile varieties are mentioned where appropriate, as are specific cultural requirements where necessary. They are grouped under Annual Grasses (hardy, followed by tender grasses), Cool Season Grasses and, the largest group of all, Warm Season Grasses.

Ethiopian fountain grass (*Pennisetum villosum*) is a warm season grass sometimes treated as a tender annual. It flowers from early summer until the frosts.

ANNUAL GRASSES

Annuals are plants that complete their whole life cycle - from seed through germination, growth, flowering and seeding - in a single growing season. Hardy annuals are those annuals which can tolerate frost. Most can be sown in autumn to overwinter in the ground and germinate in spring. Tender annuals are those annuals which cannot tolerate frost and which need to be sown or set out in the garden once all danger of frost is over. Many grasses treated in this way are perennial in frost-free climates and can be treated as such if they can be overwintered under glass where the temperature will not fall below 7° Celsius.

Hare's tail grass (*Lagurus ovatus*), like most hardy annual grasses, flowers so freely that the rather unremarkable foliage is almost hidden.

Polypogon monspeliensis

Annual beard grass (right) derives its name from the many bundles of soft, silky, jade-green bristles that surround the spikelets, making the flowerhead extraordinarily soft to the touch. The flowers are the lightest jade-green, produced over a long period from midsummer until the frosts. It self-seeds in some gardens but this is seldom regarded as a problem.

HEIGHT 60cm SPACING 15cm

Lagurus ovatus ♀

Hare's-tail grass (left) is beautiful both in the garden and for picking. The flame-shaped flowerheads seem to be densely packed with soft, beige hairs from the midst of which spring longer, less soft awns. It self-seeds on light, sandy soils and does not perform well on heavy ground. 'Nanus' is a dwarf form, growing to 15cm.

HEIGHT 60cm SPACING 15cm

Lamarckia aurea

Goldentop (right) is named for the curious way the top of the plant turns golden yellow while the bottom half stays green. The whole plant is rather stiff for a grass and it remains quaint rather than beautiful, an oddity with little landscape value, though it mixes well with other colourful annuals and bedding plants.

HEIGHT 30cm SPACING 15cm

Briza maxima

One of the most popular annual grasses, larger quaking grass (left and above) is probably among the first to be grown in gardens. It is treasured for the locket-like panicles which dance and nod in the slightest breeze. They are jade-green at first; the whole plant later ripens to palest straw colour. A British native, it can self-seed almost too freely, mainly on disturbed soils.

HEIGHT 30cm SPACING 15cm

Hordeum jubatum

Squirrel-tail grass (left) can claim to be the most colourful and showiest of the annual grasses. It flowers in early summer, making a haze of shimmering, irridescent, rosy-pink flowers until the frosts. Native to hot, stony hillsides, the plants need perfect drainage and when given these conditions may self-seed too freely. The flowers shatter as soon as picked and so are useless for arranging.

HEIGHT 30cm   SPACING 15cm

Aira elegantissima ♀

Cloud grass (above) is a delightful diminutive species with probably the tiniest spikelets of any cultivated grass. It is grown for the soft, cloud-like effect it creates, especially when planted in groups or drifts. A short-lived annual, it is best cleared once its moment of beauty is over. Cloud grass is hard to pick and dry as the gossamer-thin threads of the panicles become inextricably tangled.

HEIGHT 25cm   SPACING 15cm

Pennisetum setaceum 'Rubrum'

In purple fountain grass (above) the whole plant – leaves and flower stems – is rich burgundy red, while the flower panicles, which can be up to 30cm long and which arch dramatically, are magenta-pink at first, ripening to rich, red-ochre. They soon shatter when picked and are unsuitable for drying. Since this grass is a tender perennial usually grown as an annual, it seldom produces viable seed and is increased by division.

HEIGHT 100cm SPACING 60cm

Setaria glauca

A highly effective annual (opposite left) flowering from midsummer until the frosts, bristle grass is best planted with the sun behind it, lighting up its translucent bristles. If the flowers are intended for drying, they should be picked earlier rather than later. It is sometimes treated as a tender annual. A form with yellow bristles is also available (right).

HEIGHT 75cm SPACING 15cm

Chloris virgata

Finger grass or windmill grass (above) is curious and distinct among grasses in the stiffness of its leaves and stems. It is sometimes grown for its unique many-fingered panicles, which are excellent for drying. They can be green or purplish and, although they appear stiff, they are soft and silky to the touch.

HEIGHT 25cm SPACING 15cm

Zea mays

One of the most variable of all grasses and never found in the wild, sweet corn (maize) is available in a wide range of cultivated forms, ranging from dwarf to giant and including many with coloured cobs and/or variegated leaves. Some modern forms have been bred to perform well in the shorter, cooler summers of northern Europe. Shown here are the silks, the female flowers.

HEIGHT UP TO 240cm SPACING 60cm

Pennisetum glaucum '**Purple Majesty**'

This is an exciting new grass with leaves that become increasingly rich purple as summer advances. It bears, in late summer, a single dramatic flower. The stem later branches to produce smaller flowers at the sides.

HEIGHT 75cm SPACING 20cm

Coix lacryma-jobi

Job's tears is thought to have been grown as an ornamental in gardens since Biblical times. The grains were used to make rosaries and ornaments, and for flour in the East. It is, by modern standards, more curious than beautiful as the growth is stiff and ungainly and the leaves are coarse. But the seeds or grains are attractive, being up to 1cm long and black when mature, contrasting with the green leaves and nodding male flowers at the tips of the same stems. This grass needs a long season if it is to produce its curious grains, so it is best started in a heated greenhouse in late winter. However, it may be sown out of doors, and can self-seed, in warm climates.

HEIGHT 60cm SPACING 30cm

COOL
SEASON
GRASSES

Cool season grasses start into growth in autumn, grow throughout the winter and flower in spring or early summer. They are therefore best planted among winter- or early spring-flowering perennials, with plants grown for their foliage, or among spring and early summer bulbs. Most then become dormant or semi-dormant and so could be planted where summer flowers or grasses can grow up to conceal their off-season sulks. They can be divided or transplanted in either spring or autumn.

Sesleria heufleriana is one of the first grasses to flower, often with the last of the snowdrops. It grows to 75cm high, forming dense clumps of narrow, evergreen leaves. It tolerates sun and shade.

Calamagrostis x *acutiflora* 'Karl Foerster'

Feather reed grass is one of the most universally admired ornamental grasses, the whole plant being narrowly upright, including the flower panicles – except briefly when fully in flower, as here. Later the panicles will close up and become narrow as a pencil. 'Overdam' is a striking selection with crisply white-edged leaves but slightly smaller in growth.

HEIGHT 200cm SPACING 30cm

Briza media 'Limouzi'

Common quaking grass is a perennial quaking grass with blue-green leaves. What look like tiny lockets are the spikelets, and these pass from green to cream and finally a pale straw colour.
HEIGHT 60cm SPACING 15cm

Melica ciliata

Silky spike melic (left and above) is the showiest of the melics, treasured for the earliness of its flowering. It is ideal grown as a single specimen in smaller gardens, or as drifts where space permits. Individual plants are seldom long-lived but often seed around lightly. Grows best in sun or a little shade, in soils that do not dry out.

HEIGHT 75cm SPACING 35cm

Sesleria caerulea

Blue moor grass is grown as much for its upside-down leaves as for its black flowers with their creamy pollen sacs. Whereas in most grasses the leaves are dark above, paler beneath, in this grass the leaves are silvery blue above, green beneath, both sides being visible at the same time.

HEIGHT 20cm SPACING 10cm

Phalaris arundinacea var. picta 'Picta' ♈
Striped reed canary grass (or gardeners' garters) has
been grown in gardens since Victorian times or earlier.
The white stripes are never flushed pink. More recent
selections include 'Feesey', which is more strongly
variegated, the new growth strongly flushed pink,
'Luteopicta', striped creamy yellow in spring, and
'Streamlined', which is less variegated and fits in more
easily with other plants. All are least variegated in
summer when they should be cut down to stimulate a
flush of new leaves. They run at the root and need
controlling in all but the largest gardens. Grows
anywhere in sun or partial shade.
HEIGHT 150cm SPACING 75cm

Bouteloua gracilis

Blue grama is also known as mosquito grass for the curious way that the anthers are suspended beneath the horizontal axis of the flower, like mosquito larvae suspended beneath the surface of a sheet of water. It grows best in a sunny place, either as a specimen in a pot where its detail can be enjoyed, or naturalized in meadows.

HEIGHT 150cm SPACING 60cm

Ampelodesmos mauritanica

This dramatic grass (above) is the first of the very large grasses to flower, often with the last of the daffodils and well before *Stipa gigantea*. The flower stems, upright at first, become pendulous as the seeds mature.

HEIGHT 750cm SPACING 100cm

Alopecurus pratensis 'Aureovariegatus'

Golden foxtail grass (right) is the brightest yellow grass of spring, though duller later in the season. On light soils it may grow no more than 7.5cm tall, and may run at the root, while on heavier soils it can reach 30cm tall but remain as a clump, needing to be divided every two to three years to maintain its vigour. It flowers in late spring or early summer, after which it becomes rather drab unless cut down to provoke a new flush of leaves.

HEIGHT 30cm SPACING 20cm

Helictotrichon sempervirens ♟

Blue oat grass forms dense, rounded mounds of silvery blue, needle-like leaves that radiate from a central point. In early summer it produces flowers the same colour as the leaves, these later turning hay-coloured. Needs sun and good drainage, and dislikes both excessive summer heat and high humidity. It is inclined to foliar rust on poorly drained soils. *H. sempervirens* var. *pendulum* has gracefully arching flowering culms; 'Saphirsprudel' has bluer leaves and is less prone to rust.

HEIGHT 80cm SPACING 60cm

Arrhenatherum elatius subsp. *bulbosum* 'Variegatum'

This grass (right) has the cleanest, whitest, brightest variegation of all the smaller grasses. It is a typical cool season grass, growing through autumn and winter, flowering in spring and turning semi-dormant in summer, so is best planted where its summer garb is concealed by taller, later growers. Likes moisture-retentive soil in light shade.

HEIGHT 30cm SPACING 18cm

Festuca glauca

There are many named selections of the little blue fescue. All form dense, bun-shaped mounds and produce slender flowering spikes in early summer the same colour as their leaves. These flowers dry to hay colour and plants may look better if they are clipped off. All do best in sun on well-drained, preferably alkaline soil, and tend to sulk in excessive summer heat. They look lovely in containers or grown as ground cover. Many forms have been selected and named with slightly different foliage colours. **'Elijah Blue'** (left) is the best selection with silvery blue foliage and is larger than most. ***Festuca* 'Fromefield Blue'** (below) is a paler shade of blue and **'Festina'** (right), a new cultivar of a stronger blue. Among the best of the rest are 'Azurit' with silvery blue leaves, 'Harz' with dark olive-green leaves, and 'Golden Toupée', with unexpectedly soft yellow leaves. *F. amethystina*, *F. idahoensis* and *F. valesiaca* are similar.

HEIGHT 25cm SPACING 20cm

Milium effusum 'Aureum' ♀

In light woodland or shade, Bowles' golden grass (left) is just the right soft tint of gaudy green to go with blue-flowered spring bulbs such as scillas, muscari and bluebells, its colouring being brightly brassy in sunnier places. It is summer dormant. 'Yaffle' is more vigorous, with green-striped, pale yellow leaves.

HEIGHT 30cm SPACING 15cm

Glyceria maxima var. variegata

Striped sweet manna grass (right) is the showiest of the striped cool season grasses, its spring foliage flushed purplish pink. It does best in moist soils or shallow water where it spreads by stolons but is easily controlled. It tends to spread less in garden soil, but it should never be allowed to dry out.

HEIGHT 120cm SPACING 60cm

Elymus hispidus

Blue wheat grass (left) is the most intensely blue of all grasses, the colour so pure that other so-called blue grasses seem dowdy by comparison. It produces similarly blue wheat-like panicles which soon turn beige. Hailing from Tierra del Fuego, it grows best in cold climates, detesting hot summer nights and high humidity. *E. solandri* is almost as blue but makes low mounds, while *E. magellanicus* is far less intensely blue, virtually prostrate and only just perennial.

HEIGHT 60cm SPACING 30cm

Holcus mollis 'Albovariegatus'

Striped Yorkshire fog (above) is at its best in spring and autumn, suffering its summer dormancy with ill grace. It spreads slowly by surface runners but is easily controlled, and can make lawn-like ground cover in the right conditions. It does best on moisture-retentive soil and in some shade in hot climates.

HEIGHT 25cm SPACING 15cm

Deschampsia cespitosa

Tufted hair grass (right) is one of the key species in modern gardens, indispensable for its early flowering and continuing presence through the summer as well as for its dense tufts of dark evergreen leaves. Many selections have been named including 'Bronzeschleier', with coppery brown spikelets and 'Goldschleier', which is taller with yellow spikelets. It mixes happily with most garden plants and looks exquisite in large drifts of a single variety.

HEIGHT 90cm SPACING 60cm

Stipa gigantea ♀

Golden oats or Spanish oat grass (above) is the best-known of the 300 or so, mostly perennial, clump-forming grasses in the genus *Stipa*. Most gain their extraordinary beauty from the long awns which catch and hold the light from the sky. All need well-drained soil in sun. *Stipa gigantea* forms low mounds of dark evergreen leaves and grows 180–200cm, its tall culms and huge panicles swaying gently in the breeze. It remains eye-catching until autumn. 'Gold Fontaene' is taller (to 220cm) with larger, more golden panicles. 'Pixie' is smaller, to 150cm. Stipas should be spaced half their height apart.

Stipa pennata

European feather grass (opposite) has silvery, feathery awns 20cm long that float on the wind like a pennant. *S. barbata* and *S. pulcherrima* are similar.
HEIGHT 75cm SPACING 30cm

The panicles of the three grasses shown here are made conspicuous by their long, needle-like awns. In **Stipa turkestanica** (left) the whole plant is upright and the long, straight awns upright at first and palest jade green, becoming more spreading and slowly turning beige as summer progresses. HEIGHT 90cm SPACING 30cm

Stipa tenuissima Mexican feather grass, or pony tail grass (below right) has awns almost as long but soft as silk and thin as gossamer. The panicles are produced so freely from early until late summer – jade green at first, beige later – that the whole plant sways with the slightest suspiration of the air. It looks good well into winter. (Do not confuse with S. tenacissima, a rather coarse grass used for paper making.)
HEIGHT 60cm SPACING 30cm

Stipa calamagrostis

This grass (right) has shorter awns among the dense, arching panicles that are produced in succession throughout summer. Each panicle, at first silvery green becoming beige, only just overtops the fountain of arching foliage. It is perhaps the most graceful and free-flowering of all the middle-sized grasses. Nearly evergreen in mild climates, winter dormant in cold climates and unhappy where nights are warm and humid, this grass grows best in poor but well-drained, moisture-retentive soils. In warm climates and fertile soils it becomes uselessly floppy.

HEIGHT 90cm SPACING 60cm

WARM SEASON GRASSES

Warm season grasses do not start into growth until late spring or early summer, so they are best planted among other perennials or shrubs that flower from midsummer to autumn. They can be left standing through winter to achieve a new beauty when they are glittering with raindrops or dew, or iced with frost. They should be transplanted or divided only in spring, once they have started into growth again.

Miscanthus sinensis 'Little Kitten' is the smallest of the green-leaved eulalia grasses currently grown for their flowers. A typical warm season grass, starting into growth in late spring or early summer and flowering in early autumn, it is ideal for smaller gardens or for massing at the front of a larger planting.

Miscanthus sinensis

Coming from a huge area in the Far East, eulalia or Japanese silver grass is naturally a highly variable grass whose diversity has been increased by modern hybridizing. Both wild forms and hybrids are plants of exceptional light-catching ability and of outstanding beauty. Over 200 forms have been named, ranging from dwarf (45cm) to giant (300cm), narrow to wide-leaved, commencing flowering from midsummer till early autumn and including zebra-striped and variegated forms. All are clump-forming, frost-hardy, sun-loving and easy to grow. **'Ferner Osten'** (left) is one of the shorter varieties and is remarkable for the intensity of the flower colouring. 'Flamingo' ♀ has looser, fluffier panicles of pink and white.

HEIGHT 150cm SPACING 75cm

Miscanthus sinensis 'Poseidon'

This variety (opposite) probably has the largest panicles of any miscanthus. They are a rich, light red turning silvery with age. It boasts the lushest foliage, the leaves being broad, light green and shiny, as though glazed.

HEIGHT 220cm SPACING 100cm

Other varieties of a similar size include 'Malepartus' which many regard as the standard by which to judge all others, 'Gewitterwolke' ♀, notable for the darkness of its flowers, 'Ghana' ♀, which has pale flowers and good autumn colour, 'Kaskade' ♀, with cascading fingers to the panicles, **'Kleine Fontäne'** ♀ (left), an early flowering form, producing huge panicles, and 'Undine' ♀, the daintiest of the group. All these were awarded ♀ after recent trials at the RHS Garden, Wisley, in the UK.

Miscanthus sinensis 'Roland'

By far the tallest variety of *M. sinensis* yet introduced, mature clumps can reach over 300cm in flower. It is remarkably free-flowering, the large, open panicles being light pink, the fingers usually crimped at first.
The plant is upright but splays open under the weight of the flowers, closing up again as they turn to seed.

'Silberturm' is slightly shorter but always erect, while 'Grosse Fontäne' ♀ and 'Septemberrot' ♀ grow to about 240cm in flower, the last getting its name from the rich colouring assumed by the foliage in autumn.

HEIGHT 300cm SPACING 150cm

Miscanthus x *giganteus* 'Gotemba'

Dramatic in its combination of yellow variegation and bright red, hairy stems, 'Gotemba' is unusual in that the culms it puts on in early summer are upright, but those developed in autumn are oblique. Though shorter than its green-leaved form, it runs at the root just as vigorously.

HEIGHT 150cm SPACING 100cm

Miscanthus sinensis 'Rigoletto'

Variegated miscanthus can make a striking feature in the garden, especially when planted with the sun behind or beside them. Most often encountered is *M. sinensis* 'Variegatus' ♀ whose leaves are brightly margined and striped white. It makes a rounded mound of leaves to about 150cm wide. The variety 'Silberpfeil' is indistinguishable in its variegation but distinct in its upright habit, its greater height (180–200cm) and in losing its lower leaves, exposing its knees. **'Rigoletto'** (left) is distinctly shorter and less vigorous, making it a first choice where space is limited. 'Goldfeder' is unique in its yellow edged and striped leaves.

HEIGHT 150cm SPACING 90cm

Miscanthus sinensis 'Morning Light' ♀

Long known and grown in Japan, often as a bonsai companion plant, this is probably the oldest known cultivated variety of miscanthus (right). It is, in effect, a variegated form of *M. sinensis* 'Gracillimus', having the same narrow leaves, fine texture and rounded overall form. The narrow leaves are well variegated at close quarters but from a distance the whole plant gives a greyish effect. In warm summer climates it makes a great display of pink to reddish flowers in late summer, too late for the seeds to ripen. In cooler climates it seldom flowers when mature, though young vigorous plants sometimes do.

HEIGHT 150cm SPACING 75cm

Miscanthus sinensis 'Etincelle'

The zebra grasses, adored by the Victorians, now seem more popular than ever. The form originally introduced from Japan was *M. sinensis* 'Zebrinus' ♀ which can grow up to 240cm and is wide-spreading and often floppy in habit. 'Strictus' ♀ by contrast, is narrowly upright, densely clump-forming, grows to 200cm and has smaller, more freely produced bands. Both 'Kirk Alexander' and 'Pünktchen' are excellent in hot summers, but do not stripe well in cool seasons. **'Etincelle'** (opposite) is a new variety remarkable for its narrow leaves, the freedom of its flowering and because the bands seldom show any scorching. 'Hinjo' and 'Tiger Cub' are dwarf varieties ideal for smaller gardens, growing to about 140cm in flower.

HEIGHT 150cm SPACING 90cm

Miscanthus nepalensis

Instantly recognizable by its honey-coloured flowers, other miscanthus having reddish, pink or silvery flowers, this is often said to be the most desirable of all miscanthus (opposite). Early introductions were of quite short plants, to less than 100cm in flower, and decidedly frost tender, but more recent introductions are taller, more vigorous and seemingly hardier.

HEIGHT 150cm SPACING 90cm

Miscanthus transmorrisonensis

Distinct among miscanthus in being virtually evergreen, this is almost as variable as *M. sinensis*, having narrow-leaved and some wider-leaved forms, as well as a zebra-striped form, as yet unnamed. The flowers are produced over a long season and are held well clear of the leaf mound.

HEIGHT 200cm SPACING 80cm

Miscanthus sinensis var. *condensatus* 'Cosmopolitan' ♔

Both this cultivar (left) and 'Cabaret' (above) are dramatically variegated selections of the coastal form of eulalia grass, *M. sinensis*, var. *condensatus*. They have wider leaves (as much as 4cm across), stouter stems and greater vigour but are slightly more tender. Mature specimens of 'Cosmopolitan' are among the most spectacular of all garden plants. In warm summer climates the showy flowers can be carried high above the foliage, but in cooler climates they scarcely appear above it, if at all. Occasional green shoots should be cut out. Several green-leaved reversions have been named but they should all be known as 'Cosmo Revert'.

HEIGHT 270cm SPACING 120cm

Miscanthus sinensis var. condensatus 'Cabaret'

While other variegated grasses have the white stripe at the margin, 'Cabaret' is, uniquely, centrally variegated (left). The variegation is more pronounced in hot summer climates than in cool ones, but it is still one of the most sumptuous and showy grasses for cool climates. Every bit as bold and spectacular as 'Cosmopolitan' ♀, it is generally slightly shorter in growth, and makes wider clumps. It seldom flowers in the UK.

HEIGHT 220cm SPACING 140cm

Miscanthus sacchariflorus

Among the largest of ornamental grasses and opulently leafy, silver banner grass (right) is grown in cool summer gardens, where it seldom flowers, for its subtropical luxuriance. In warm summer climates its slender flower plumes add extra charm. Unlike other miscanthus, *M. sacchariflorus* runs vigorously at the root and so is useful for binding slopes and planting large areas, but it is difficult to control in smaller gardens. In the wild this species grows in wet places.

HEIGHT 240cm SPACING 150cm

Molinia caerulea subsp. caerulea 'Heidebraut'

Heather bride (left) is fairly typical of the purple moor grasses, though slightly bigger than most at 100cm tall. The moor grasses are clump forming and wholly deciduous – that is, the stems and leaves break off from the roots cleanly once frosted, which most grasses do not. In the wild they grow on wet, often acid, heaths and moorlands across Europe and Asia but they seem happy enough in garden soil. In cultivation the species divides into two groups: purple moor grasses (*M. caerulea* subsp. *caerulea*) with varieties growing no more than 100cm, and *M. caerulea* subsp. *arundinacea* (see pages 100–101) with varieties up to 240cm. All are grown for their structural form, either upright, like 'Heidebraut', or arching, as in varieties like 'Strahlenquelle', and for their delicate panicles.

HEIGHT 100cm SPACING 45cm

Molinia caerulea subsp. caerulea 'Edith Dudszus'

Another upright variety (left) of the subspecies *caerulea*, but remarkable for the intensity of the panicles' colouring, which is almost black. Like most moor grasses, the whole plant turns an intense yellow in autumn.

HEIGHT 90cm SPACING 45cm

Molinia caerulea subsp. caerulea 'Variegata' ♀

This is one of the most familiar of garden grasses and a long-time favourite (above). It is treasured for its cream variegation, a colouring that suffuses the stems and even the panicles of this variety. 'Carmarthen' is similar but the variegation is white, the stems green and the flowers presented in a narrower panicle; the effect is less bright than that of 'Variegata'. 'Claerwen' is similar but more subtly coloured and distinct in its narrow, almost black, panicles.

HEIGHT 45cm SPACING 20cm

Molinia caerulea subsp. arundinacea 'Windspiel'

Like all the varieties of subspecies *arundinacea*, 'Windspiel' is grown for its ability to behave like a living sculpture in the garden: tall and stately at rest, the stems, topped by their diffuse panicles, move gracefully with the slightest stirrings of a breeze and dance when the wind blows. The sculptural qualities are seen best when these grasses are grown as single plants in the midst of a carpet of lower-growing perennials or grasses, while the elegance of their panicles is displayed to advantage when back- or side-lit in front of a dark background. Similarly upright are 'Bergfreund' and 'Skyracer'.

HEIGHT 240cm SPACING 75cm

Molinia caerulea subsp. *arundinacea* 'Transparent'

This variety is named for the transparent section between the top of the leaf mound and the bottom of the panicle, making it easy to see through between the slender flowering stems; the name could apply equally well to any of this subspecies. It is even more remarkable for the darkness of the individual spikelets, and for the way the flowering stems arch under the weight of the panicles, almost touching the ground when wet with rain and springing up again when dry. 'Fontäne' and 'Karl Foerster' have similarly arching flowering stems, while those of 'Zuneigung' bend even further, having larger, heavier spikelets.

HEIGHT 240cm SPACING 75cm

Panicum virgatum 'Warrior'

The panic or switch grasses are natives of the vanishing tallgrass prairie. They are grown in gardens for the billowing cloud-like effects of their diffuse panicles, beset with myriads of tiny purple spikelets. In this variety (left) the flowers are reddish pink in late summer, the panicles exceptionally large and showy. 'Squaw' is a sister seedling, similar but more lax in its growth. Both have green leaves assuming rich golden autumn colours. Similarly green-leaved are 'Northwind' (150cm), which forms narrowly upright clumps, 'Red Cloud' (150cm), with distinctly red flowers and purplish autumn colour and 'Shenandoah' (120cm), with rich burgundy-red autumn colour. These varieties are all drought tolerant once established.

HEIGHT 150cm SPACING 75cm

Panicum virgatum 'Dallas Blues'

Outstanding for the intense blueness of the foliage and flowering culms, and the contrasting soft pink of its flowers, this is a vigorous variety growing to 180cm (right). Other blue panic grasses include 'Blue Tower', 'Cloud Nine' (both 240cm) and 'Prairie Sky' (120cm), which is extremely blue but rather lax in habit unless grown on sharply drained, poor soils. None of these blue varieties takes on the glorious golden autumn tints of the green-leaved forms. The panic grasses can be massed or used as isolated specimens, and hold their form well when dried, making them excellent subjects for arranging.

HEIGHT 180cm SPACING 90cm

Pennisetum villosum ♀

Ethiopian fountain grass or feathertop (below) is a short-lived perennial sometimes treated as an annual in cold climates. This species is grown for the succession of almost white feathery flowers produced from earliest summer until the frosts. It tends to make a rather untidy mound of foliage, wider than it is high, the flowers being produced on rather lax stems. Nonethless it is highly desirable, massed or on its own, and is valued as a cut flower for arranging, both in the green and dried.

HEIGHT 60cm SPACING 60cm

Pennisetum macrourum

South African fountain grass (above) is an invaluable grass for drawing the eye. The pencil-thin, spike-like panicles, produced at eye level, catch and hold the luminescence from the sky, making them often the most luminous items in a planting. Coming from South Africa this lovely grass is not totally frost hardy in colder climates. It appears to form dense clumps, but then sends out runners, at the ends of which further clumps are produced. (It is often confused with *P. incomptum* which is shorter, has fatter, less stiffly erect panicles and runs at the root, forming dense drifts or patches.)

HEIGHT 180cm SPACING 80cm

Pennisetum alopecuroides

One of the most valuable ornamental grass species, fountain grass (opposite) is grown for its dense, cylindrical, foxy-red, spike-like panicles. These are carried on slender stems that arch under their weight and are borne above dense clumps of narrow, dark green foliage. Flowering can begin as early as midsummer in warm climates, but in cool summer climates often does not start until early autumn. The panicles, if wanted for arranging, should be picked before they are fully opened; left on the plant, they shatter earlier in winter than those of many other ornamental grasses. 'Hameln' is a dwarf variety that often starts flowering earlier than the species itself (height 45cm, spacing 30cm). 'Little Bunny' is miniature at 20cm, spacing 15cm.

HEIGHT 90cm SPACING 75cm

Pennisetum alopecuroides '**Moudry**'

Black-flowered fountain grass (left) is grown for its extraordinarily dark flowers. This is not an easy grass to grow successfully as it needs long, hot summers to flower well. In cool climates the flowers often do not fully emerge from the surrounding foliage before the frosts, while in hot summers it usually flowers freely enough but then seeds itself excessively. This can, however, be forestalled by cutting off the flowerheads before the seed ripens.

HEIGHT 60cm SPACING 60cm

Pennisetum orientale '**Tall Tails**'

While this form of oriental fountain grass (below) is very distinct, it has all the grace and long-flowering qualities characteristic of the species. It is exceptionally tall and free-flowering, moving gracefully in any wind.

HEIGHT 180cm SPACING 75cm

Pennisetum orientale 'Karley Rose'

This cultivar is the most richly coloured of the oriental fountain grasses, the flowers almost red in bud, opening to a rich pink, produced in long, elegant spires. These grasses flower over an extremely long period, from midsummer until the frosts. It is tall for an oriental fountain grass; the species itself grows to no more than 30–45cm in flower. Both are showy enough to grow as specimens and are effective when massed too. Oriental fountain grass dislikes being divided, so established clumps should not be split into more than three or four pieces. It is also depth sensitive, so ensure the crown is not buried.

HEIGHT 120cm SPACING 45cm

Cortaderia richardii ♀

New Zealand pampas or tussock grass is quite different from the more familiar South American pampas grasses, both in character and cultural requirements. This species is native to damp, wet and even seasonally inundated open spaces throughout New Zealand. In gardens it grows best with plenty of moisture, as beside a pond or stream, or in soil enriched with organic matter. It flowers from early summer, the plumes staying attractive until early winter.
HEIGHT 300cm SPACING 150cm

Cortaderia selloana

The pampas grasses have the largest, showiest flower plumes of any frost hardy grass (below). The plumes are often of a startling whiteness that can make them difficult to place in the garden. On the whole they look most at home grown among other large plants, whether grasses, shrubs or perennials, or else in large, open spaces with the sun beyond or beside them, set against a background of sable pines. The species is variable and it is worth buying named forms such as 'Sunningdale Silver' ♀, 'Monstrosa' or 'Pumila' ♀, which is dwarf at 150cm in flower. None is free-flowering until well established. The leaves are edged with backward-pointing teeth which can cut to the bone; handle with care.

HEIGHT 300cm SPACING 150cm

Cortaderia selloana 'Albolineata'

The white-variegated pampas grasses (above) have the merit of being attractive throughout the year, not just while in bloom. This is one of the smaller variegated selections at 150cm in flower, while 'Silver Comet' grows almost as tall as the best green-leaved varieties. 'Aureolineata' ♀ is gold-variegated, and strong growing, reaching 240cm in flower.

HEIGHT 150cm SPACING 120cm

Calamagrostis x acutiflora 'Overdam'

Striped feather reed grass (right) is a chimeral sport of *C. x acutiflora* 'Karl Foerster', differing not only in its white-striped leaves, flushed pink at first, but also in its lesser stature. The variegation is brightest on strongly growing plants, but fades as the season goes on. If cut down in midsummer, a new flush of foliage will be more brightly variegated. It can suffer from foliar rusts in hot, humid climates.

HEIGHT 120cm SPACING 90cm

Calamagrostis brachytricha

Coming into flower in early autumn, Korean feather reed grass (below) is one of the finest varieties for winter effect, the whole plant remaining in good heart almost until the spring and taking on a whole new significance when crusted with frost and spangled with snow. While it is one of the best garden grasses, it is also excellent for arranging. Panicles, purple-tinted at first,

Calamagrostis x acutiflora 'Karl Foerster'

Feather reed grass (above) is a key landscaping grass, grown for its early flowering, the length of time it contributes to the garden and for its extraordinarily upright habit. This is invaluable where a vertical accent is wanted. The flowers emerge in early summer, thin as a pencil, fluff out to flower, revealing tints of pink and purple, then close up again, narrow as a pipe cleaner. A sterile natural hybrid of European origin, it is particularly appropriate where the possibility of grasses seeding into the wild is a worry.

HEIGHT 180cm SPACING 75cm

fade to light silvery grey and later to burnt umber. Unlike the more familiar 'Karl Foerster', the panicles remain feathery even when dried. It is more shade tolerant than many.

HEIGHT 120cm SPACING 75cm

Calamagrostis emodensis

Differing from other cultivated reed grasses in its pendulous, not upright, plumes, this easily grown grass (opposite) comes into flower in high summer. It is effective in the garden and for arranging, both green and dry, though its value in the garden does not last as long as most ornamental grasses.

HEIGHT 180cm SPACING 75cm

Bromus aleutensis

Few bromes are grown in gardens, but the Aleutian brome (left) is outstanding for the elegance of its pendulous green panicles and for its ability to grow in shade as well as in sun. A native of North America from the Aleutian Islands down to the Olympic Mountains, it dislikes summer heat and is easily grown in most soils. It is ideal for arranging, fresh or dry, losing little of its colouring when dry. Like most bromes, it will seed itself about lightly when it is happily situated.

HEIGHT 80cm SPACING 30cm

Hystrix patula

Bottlebrush grass (right) is sometimes called porcupine grass, which is the meaning of its Latin generic name. This is a short-lived perennial grass native to damp woodlands and meadows. In cultivation it grows best in moisture-retentive soils, in sun or light shade, but it is not happy in hot gardens. Though the panicles are striking at close quarters, making them ideal for arranging, they tend to be rather insignificant in the garden, their colouring blending in with the general green of other vegetation.

HEIGHT 90cm SPACING 30cm

Saccharum arundinaceum

Relatively new to cultivation, this strong-growing grass, hardy sugar cane, is grown in the USA for its spectacular flowers. In much of northern continental Europe, where it seems unlikely to flower, it is valued for its huge clumps of tropical-looking foliage. The individual leaves are broad and grey with a clean white midrib, forming upright spreading clumps over 200cm tall. The showy panicles resemble the elongated plumes of pampas grass; they are pink at first, maturing to silvery grey.

HEIGHT 280cm or more in flower, 200cm in leaf SPACING 100cm

Chasmanthium latifolium

Wood oats or river oats (above and right) is one of the few grasses that thrives in shade, even dry shade, which is unexpected since it is native to damp woodlands. Its charms are subtle rather than showy, the spikelets having every appearance of having been ironed and polished, or carved from mahogany. It flowers best in cool climates when grown in sun, though the best foliage is produced in shade, especially in hot summer areas. Although the individual panicles are ideal for arranging, this grass is most effective in the garden, grown in groups or drifts.

HEIGHT 90cm SPACING 30cm

Imperata cylindrica 'Rubra'

Japanese blood grass is the most dramatically coloured of all ornamental grasses, especially when grown so that the sun can shine through its leaves. This was grown in Japan as a bonsai companion plant for more than a century before reaching the West. It does best in moisture-retentive soils in sun and is surprisingly slow to increase. (It should never be confused with *I. cylindrica* var. *major* which is an aggressively spreading, sand-dune-binding tropical grass whose sale is now restricted in the USA.)

HEIGHT 38cm SPACING 15cm

Hakonechloa macra 'Alboaurea' ♀

Golden Hakone grass is one of the most brightly variegated of all grasses. It is named for Mount Hakone, in Japan's main island Honshu, the region where it grows in the wild. This grass is treasured for the cascading habit of its leaves, which perfectly complements the shape of a traditional terracotta pot, as much as for its colouring. 'Alboaurea' has leaves striped green and yellow, and flecked with white and vinous red, whereas the similar 'Aureola' ♀ is merely green and yellow striped. The cultivar 'Albovariegata' is white-variegated in strong sunlight, but cream-variegated in cooler ones. The colouring is most garish in sun, more subtle in shade, and the single species and its varieties grow best in damp, moisture-retentive soils.

HEIGHT 30cm SPACING 20cm

Eragrostis species

This newly introduced species (RCB RA-X 2), recently collected in cloud forest in Argentina, has deep green leaves that look as though they have been fashioned from the finest possible velvet, making it a marvellous plant for foliage or texture gardening. The flowers are large, diffuse panicles, resembling giant panicles of *Stipa tenuissima*.

HEIGHT 120cm SPACING 75cm

Setaria palmifolia

Quite different from the *Setaria* species grown in gardens for the showy flowerheads, such as *S. macrostachya* or *S. italica*, palm grass is grown for its deeply pleated leaves. The flowers, being small and green, are of little ornamental merit. It is usually considered frost tender and recommended for use in conservatories and for standing or planting out in summer, but it has proved hardy in southern England over many years. Several species, including *S. chevalieri*, *S. megaphylla*, *S. paniculifera*, *S. poiretiana* and *S. pumila*, are similar. The plant cultivated in Britain may be different from that grown in the USA.

HEIGHT 100cm SPACING 75cm

Andropogon gerardii

Big blue-stem, or turkey foot, is
called 'big' because in its native
prairies it was reputed to grow
taller than a man on horseback,
and turkey foot because the few-
fingered flowers have a fancied
resemblance to a turkey's foot. It
bears scant resemblance to little
blue-stem (see page 120), though
they were once in the same genus.
Grown more for its foliage than its
flowers, the leaves and stems are
powder-blue in high summer, the
tips of the leaves becoming stained
with purple late in the year, the
whole plant turning a rich sienna in
the winter. Grows best in a sunny,
well-drained position.

HEIGHT 180cm SPACING 50cm

119

Schizachyrium scoparium

Few grasses change as much through the season as little blue-stem (opposite), once one of the hallmark plants of the tallgrass prairie. The narrow leaves start the season grey, becoming blue in high summer and take on, as autumn approaches, rich vinous-purple tints, finally changing for the winter to a unique shade of foxy-red, a richer colour than that of any other grass. The tiny flowers often pass unnoticed unless back- or side-lit against a darker background. It is strictly clump-forming. 'The Blues' is a selection with notably blue summer foliage.

HEIGHT 75cm SPACING 30cm

Cynodon aethiopicus

Star grass (right) is a little charmer in a genus of otherwise rather weedy and aggressive grasses. The unusual flowerheads are interesting in the detail but exert no great attraction from a distance. An East African native, it needs to be grown in well-drained soil in a sunny position.

HEIGHT 30cm SPACING 30cm

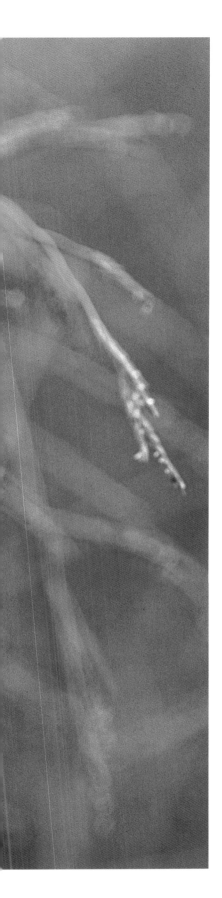

Melica altissima 'Atropurpurea'

But for the glory of its richly coloured panicles, loved by flower arrangers, purple Siberian melic (below) would hardly warrant a place in the garden. A native of woodland margins, it has an untidy, sprawling habit, often leaning on neighbours for support. Its season of beauty is short compared with that of other grasses and by midsummer, even in southern England, it becomes semi-dormant, while in hotter climates it is totally summer dormant. This melic is lovely in arrangements, fresh or dried, if picked before the flowers open.

HEIGHT 120cm SPACING 30cm

Eragrostis 'Wind Dance'

This form (above) of Elliott's lovegrass (*E. elliottii*) has been selected for its freedom of flower, the flowering stems being more upright than those of *E. curvula*, and therefore more showy. The plumes open in midsummer and mature to a tan colour as the seeds ripen, then turn a lighter straw colour for the winter. It needs to be grown in full sun and is very drought tolerant, but it needs perfect drainage and will not tolerate winter wet.

HEIGHT 120cm SPACING 75cm

Eragrostis curvula

African lovegrass (left) is one of the most finely textured and graceful of all grasses. The narrow, grey-green leaves are almost hidden by the violet flowers when they appear in huge, arching panicles in mid- to late summer. Evergreen in warm winter areas, it is usually cut to the ground in colder districts, though it often assumes some autumn colour before fading. It self-seeds freely, especially where planted on disturbed ground.

HEIGHT 90cm SPACING 45cm

Chionochloa rubra

Red tussock grass or red snow grass (above) is unusual in being more conspicuous in winter than summer; it is the only frost-hardy true grass to have brown leaves. It makes tight, upright spreading tussocks of stiff, slightly arching leaves of a distinct coppery-bronze. Among these, the flowering stems and panicle branches seem to disappear, leaving the apparently disembodied pale spikelets hovering above the clump. It grows best in damp or moisture-retentive soils in sun and associates well with greys and silvers.

HEIGHT 180cm SPACING 100cm

Phragmites australis 'Variegatus'

While the wild form of the common reed is an aggressively spreading binder of river banks and marshy ground, this variegated form (striped common reed, above).spreads relatively little when grown in sun in garden soil. It only spreads rapidly when grown beside water. This reed can be effective grown in a submerged container, happy with up to 10cm of water over its roots.

HEIGHT 240cm SPACING 100cm

Anemanthele lessoniana

Pheasant, gossamer or wind grass (right), formerly *Stipa arundinacea*, comes from New Zealand. It derives its common name from the similarity of its foliage colour to that of a pheasant, the colour being most intense in plants grown in poor soils or starved in pots. The flowers are produced on gossamer-thin, claret-coloured stems in large, loose panicles that are largely lost among the leaves. It will grow in sun or shade, wet or dry, and seeds around lightly in suitable soils, making excellent ground cover. Where grown in large drifts the planting will ripple in the wind like waves running across a field of corn.

HEIGHT 90cm SPACING 60cm

Arundo donax 'Golden Chain'

Gold-striped provencal reed (above left) is a relatively new introduction, differing from *A. donax* var. *versicolor* (below left) not only in its gold, rather than white, variegation but also in its much smaller stature.

HEIGHT 150cm SPACING 90cm

Arundo donax var. versicolor

The provencal reed (*A. donax*) is the largest, most architecturally impressive of all frost-hardy grasses, and *A. donax* var. *versicolor* (left) is a dramatic variegated form, its leaves and stems boldly white-striped. In cold winter climates the striped provencal reed (or striped giant reed) can be grown as a conservatory plant but elsewhere it can be grown out of doors, being cut to the ground by frosts in areas with cool summers; where summers are hotter, it may survive with little winter damage. Several forms are in cultivation, varying in the boldness of their variegation, and some are hardier than others.

HEIGHT 240cm SPACING 100cm

Spartina pectinata 'Aureomarginata'

Striped prairie cord grass (left) is grown for the graceful arching habit of its gold-edged leaves. The flowers, produced in late summer well above the leaf mound, lack the light-capturing qualities of most ornamental grasses. A native of marshlands and wet prairies, where it spreads rapidly by cord-like rhizomes, it grows well in garden soil, where its spreading habit will be curbed.

HEIGHT 210cm SPACING 90cm

Leymus arenarius

Blue lyme grass or dune grass (right) is treasured for its bold, intensely blue foliage. This is not the easiest grass to accommodate in gardens because of its aggressively spreading habit, which makes it ideal to bind sand dunes. It can run as much as 240cm in all directions in one season. It was used by Gertrude Jekyll, who liked to grow it with pink roses, but in modern gardens it is often grown in pots to control its spread. The flowers are wheat-like spikes, the same colour as the foliage.

HEIGHT 120cm SPACING 100cm

Sedges, rushes & cat-tails

Though generally grass-like in appearance, sedges, rushes and cat-tails are in fact separated from the true grasses by aeons of evolutionary time and differ from them in details of their leaves and flowers, as well as in their general cultural requirements. The sedges are a large family containing several genera of diverse plants mostly from the cool temperate regions, enjoying cooler and usually damper conditions than the true grasses. The rushes are a smaller family with relatively few garden-worthy plants, though the woodrushes, which belong here, are often decorative as well as useful. The cat-tails, reedmaces or bulrushes are a family of a single genus, with only ten species of aquatic or marginal plants with conspicuous flowerheads.

Right *Carex elata* 'Aurea' ♀, a sedge; far right top *Juncus patens* 'Carman's Gray', a rush; far right below *Typha angustifolia*, a reedmace

128

Carex pendula 'Moonraker'

This dramatically variegated form of common
pendulous sedge (above) performs best in cool
climates where a succession of new, variegated
leaves is produced through the growing season.
In warmer climates the variegation may only be
apparent in spring, the later leaves being green;
in hot climates it may not show any variegation
at all. Where it thrives it may seed around, most
seedlings being similarly variegated. It is less
vigorous than the green-leaved form, but also
less architectural. It grows best in shade and in
moist soil or under no more than 10cm of water.
HEIGHT 75cm SPACING 60cm

Carex oshimensis 'Variegata'

Cultivated since Victorian times, originally as a house plant, this lovely sedge (left) is versatile in the garden, either in pots or as an accent plant, grown singly or in drifts. It comes into its own in winter, making a bright patch of colour when associated with bergenias, whose leaves are red in winter. It grows best in cool conditions, needing shade in hot summer areas. The cream leaf colouring is variable, and more yellow or more nearly white selections can be made simply by dividing plants showing variation.

HEIGHT 40cm SPACING 30cm

Carex comans 'Frosted Curls'

New Zealand hair sedge or blonde sedge (left below) has variable colouring in the wild, being sometimes red, brown, tawny or green, but the curling tips to the leaves distinguish it from other sedges. 'Frosted Curls' was a chance find in a wild population, remarkable for its almost white appearance. Some plants sold under this name are seedlings; they lack the leaves' soft touch, typical of the true plant. It enjoys well-drained, moisture-retentive soil in sun or shade.

HEIGHT 30cm SPACING 30cm

Carex phyllocephala 'Sparkler'

The name 'phyllocephala' means that the leaves are collected together in a head at the top of the stem, giving this sedge (right) a superficial resemblance to an umbrella plant (*Cyperus*). A native of China, this striking variegated form originated in Japan. It enjoys moisture-retentive soil in light shade, and survives winters outdoors in southern England. In colder areas it makes a superb container plant. Green-leaved seedlings occasionally appear, hardier than the variegated form.

HEIGHT 60cm SPACING 15cm

Cyperus papyrus ♟

Egyptian paper reed (right) is the papyrus of the ancients and the bulrush of the Bible. This extraordinary plant has no basal leaves, their photosynthetic function being carried out by the tall stems and the filaments of the huge, spherical inflorescences, which can be over 30cm across. It spreads by means of tough rhizomes, needing a minimum winter temperature of 15° C, below which the growth buds fail to mature. It grows best in saturated soil or with up to 15cm of water over the roots.

HEIGHT 300cm SPACING 100cm

Uncinia rubra

Hook sedges (below) are the Antipodean cousins of Old World sedges. They differ in that the seed tips terminate in a stiff bristle that turns back on itself to form a hook which catches on the fur of passing animals to aid distribution. Grown in gardens for their richly coloured foliage, they like moist but well-drained soils in light shade; the leaves may be less well-coloured in too much shade.

HEIGHT 25cm SPACING 25cm

Schoenoplectus lacustris 'Zebrinus'

Zebra clubrush (above), an aquatic plant, is often mistaken for a rush but it is, in fact, a sedge; the leaves have been replaced by stems. Both this and the variety 'Albescens', in which the stems appear almost wholly white, contrast dramatically with the rounded leaves of water lilies, lotus plants and many other aquatics. 'Golden Sword' is a selection with all-gold stems. The stems of young plants are often broken by wind and weather, but this seldom happens with well-established clumps. It grows best in saturated soil or in water with no more than 7cm over the roots.

HEIGHT 150cm SPACING 100cm

Cyperus involucratus ♡

The umbrella plant (above) is grown as much for its architectural qualities as for its rich, shiny green stems and foliage. This loses none of its appeal through being widely popular as a house plant, as well as in ponds. 'Nanus' is a dwarf form and 'Variegatus' an inconstant form with more or less white-striped leaves. None is particularly frost hardy. Plants need dividing from time to time as they grow out from the centre, leaving dead space in the middle. Viviparous by nature, they can readily be increased by placing inverted whorls of leaves in a saucer of water. It likes moist or saturated soil, or having up to 15cm of water over its roots.
HEIGHT 100cm SPACING 30cm

Luzula nivea

Snowy woodrush (left) is quite different from the common woodrush, *L. sylvatica*. It forms narrow tufts of upright leaves, thinly covered in white hairs, and produces dingy, off-white flowers in summer. It can make effective ground cover in shade, among rhododendrons or other shade-tolerant shrubs.

HEIGHT 60cm SPACING 30cm

Luzula sylvatica 'Aurea'

Common woodrush is found in the northern hemisphere in damp or dry woodland. Golden woodrush (right) is grown for the intensity of its winter colouring, the summer leaves being yellowish green. 'Taggart's Cream' has bright white leaves in early spring; these fade through cream to green by midsummer. All grow best in shade in rich, damp soils but will also tolerate dry conditions, even dry shade.

HEIGHT 60cm SPACING 30cm

Juncus effusus f. spiralis

Curly common rush (opposite) is one of several corkscrew rushes, the curling leaves a juvenile characteristic of the genus that has become fixed in several species. Others include *J. balticus* 'Spiralis' which runs slowly at the root, *J. conglomeratus* 'Spiralis', miniature at 15cm, and *J. inflexus* 'Afro' which grows in ordinary garden soil. The others grow best in wet or saturated soil, or with their crowns covered by 5–10cm of water.

HEIGHT 75cm SPACING 60cm

Typha angustifolia

Slender reedmace (right) is one of the few cat-tails, with *T. minima*, polite enough to be admitted to most gardens. The majority of species, like the common bulrush *T. latifolia* (see page 25), are rampantly aggressive and fit only for large landscapes. This is grown in ponds for the elegance of its narrow leaves and stems. The thin maces are excellent for arranging but should be sprayed with hair lacquer to delay shattering; a single seedhead can contain 100,000 kapok-like seeds.

HEIGHT 200cm SPACING 100cm

caring for grasses

While grasses generally give more beauty for less work than any other sort of plant, there are certain practical considerations to be borne in mind when buying, siting and maintaining grasses. These are explained in general terms in the following pages but, where a particular grass has specific needs, these are covered in the plant's description in the Gallery of Grasses (pages 54–135).

Even the seedheads of grasses, like these *Stipa barbata* shown here, have an ethereal beauty.

How you approach the choice of grasses for your garden will depend largely on whether you are at heart a designer looking for a plant to fulfil a particular role, a plantsman looking for plants to increase your plant knowledge or simply a carefree gardener buying on a whim. Such decisions are purely a matter of personal choice, but there are practical considerations too, and these are matters of principle. The grass you choose will only flourish if you plant it in a suitable garden habitat, and the matching of a plant to its place in the garden is the soundest way of ensuring its success. Such is the variety of ornamental grasses available today that it is possible to find one or several grasses suited to almost every garden situation.

choosing, buying and siting

The most important aspects of a garden habitat are climate and soil. The severity or temperance of a climate is determined mainly by the coldness of its winters and it is helpful to know the relative coldness of your locality in order to choose grasses that will succeed in it. Summer heat may be as important a factor in the winter hardiness of plants as cold. Warm season grasses that have been well-ripened by summer heat can generally tolerate lower winter temperatures than those that have not. For example, the striped provencal reed, *Arundo donax* 'Versicolor', is seldom hardy outdoors in northern Europe though it survives much colder winters in parts of America. Heat can also affect a grass's flowering: bushy beard grass (*Andropogon glomeratus*) and Elliott's broom sedge (*A. gyrans*), though perfectly frost hardy in the average climate of southern England, never flower there because of the lack of summer heat. But heat may not be an unmixed blessing. Some cool season grasses grown in a hot climate may expire during a relatively mild winter if they have been weakened by the summer heat.

Rainfall, or the lack of it, can also be a limiting factor. Generally the true grasses do not do well in areas of very high rainfall, such as the Lake District and coastal Cornwall in the UK, and parts of the Pacific Northwest in the USA. The sedges and rushes do better in such conditions. Equally, grasses do not flourish in arid conditions, though most can tolerate considerable summer dryness. A few, such as porcupine grass (*Festuca punctoria*) and *Muhlenbergia rigens* have adapted through evolution to growing in arid areas.

Most grasses will grow reasonably well in any fertile (but not too fertile) soil, and relatively few are bothered by whether the soil is acidic or alkaline. Exceptions include *Koeleria glauca* and *Melica ciliata* which will flourish on chalk soils where few other grasses will succeed, and *Deschampsia flexuosa*, which does best on acid soils, though these can, of course, be grown on other soils as well. More important is whether or not the soil is well drained, for few will tolerate

The widest range of ornamental grasses is usually available only from specialist nurseries but most garden centres offer an exciting selection of reliable, time-tried and trusted varieties, as well as novelties. The plants are usually clearly labelled with essential information about their cultural needs. Most are firm in their pots and are sold at sizes that ensure they establish quickly once planted. The greatest choice is usually found in spring although the showiest grasses generally perform in late summer.

poorly drained soils for long. In terms of soil texture, some grasses do better in certain soils than others: *Calamagrostis* x *acutiflora* 'Karl Foerster', *Deschampsia cespitosa* and cultivars, *Elymus hispidus* and *Phalaris arundinacea* and cultivars do particularly well on heavy clay soils, and *Spartina pectinata* and *Holcus mollis* 'Albovariegatus' thrive on light, sandy soils.

It is always worth checking that the grass you are buying suits the purpose for which you intend it – a small grass for an alpine situation, a shade-tolerant grass for a woodland area and so on. This information can usually be found on the label, but failing that it is worth asking the nursery or garden centre staff.

BUYING

Ornamental grasses are now available in considerable variety from nurseries and garden centres, though often the newer and rarer varieties may be obtainable only from specialist nurseries, and often only by mail order.

When buying grasses from a retail outlet it is important to check the quality of the plant for yourself. The first thing to verify is the variety, and that the grass is suitable for the intended garden habitat. If the plant is not labelled, or if you are unsure that it is correctly labelled, there is usually someone on hand who can advise you. Next, check that the plant looks healthy and worth the price asked. A well-grown grass should fill about two-thirds of the pot and should be growing vigorously, with no dead or withered leaves. The foliage should be turgid – that is, not limp or floppy – and of a good, healthy green; if it is a variegated variety, the green portions of the leaves should be of a good green. Nor should the leaves be withered at the tips, a sign that the plant has been through a period of water deprivation. A few grasses, particularly cool season growers like striped bulbous oat grass (*Arrhenatherum elatius* subsp. *bulbosum* 'Variegatum'), are sometimes infected by fungal rust which can be seen as little coral-coloured spots on the leaves. These are due to poor growing conditions and it is best to avoid such plants as they could spread the fungus to other grasses. Plants that seem to be ailing in their pots in the nursery will generally look poorly in the garden.

Finally, you should tip the grass out of its pot and inspect the roots. This is particularly important if buying grasses in the spring, before they have put on their full complement of leaves. While the pot should not be filled with roots, there should be sufficient to bind the growing mix. If the potting compost falls away from the roots as soon as you tip it out, either the plant has been recently potted on into a larger size of pot, or the roots have been eaten, for example by vine weevil. The roots of grasses are fibrous, usually brown, but the actively growing tips are usually white, and these should be visible around the outside of the potting compost. If the compost appears to be held together by a dense hairnet of fine brown roots without any white growing tips, the grass has probably been in its pot too long and may be difficult to establish; there will usually be other indicators in the top growth, such as dead or withered leaves. Avoid grasses that are growing in their pots to an accompaniment of weeds as the latter will be more likely to flourish in your garden than the grass. Avoid also those grasses that are light when you pick them up: the growing mix will have dried out and may be difficult to re-wet. Avoid cut-price grasses: there is usually a good reason for their cheapness.

When buying by mail order you are, in effect, buying blind, and if you are not happy with the plants from one mail order source, try another. Recommendation by a friend is often the best way to locate a reliable mail order source, reliability being the sending out of plants of good quality true to their name. Some mail order nurseries send out bare-rooted plants and these should be dealt with as soon as they are received. Soak the roots for a few hours to ensure that the

When buying grasses, ensure that the leaves are turgid and vigorous (top). Tip the grass out of its pot to check root growth (above): there should be many vigorous white roots.

Growing young grasses raised from seed or division in plugs encourages them to make deep roots. Plugs are an ideal way to add ornamental grasses to meadows, or to grow on in larger pots to set out in the garden later.

grasses are turgid, then plant them straight away. With small plants it may be better to establish them in containers in a protected place before setting them out in the garden.

In general, smaller plants establish more quickly than larger specimens, though plainly there will be occasions when larger plants may be more appropriate, as when one needs a specimen plant or is using a grass as a focal point in a bedding scheme or in a container.

It is also possible to buy grasses as plugs or liners. Plugs are very small plants, usually grown by wholesalers in trays of 20 or 30 for sale to retailers who pot them into larger pots and grow them on for sale. Liners are similar but usually a little larger. Plugs are sometimes used as a way of introducing extra grass species into meadows, but they establish best in areas of the garden where they are free from competition. They are worth considering where large quantities of grasses are needed: they can either be moved into larger pots to be grown on or else be grown on in nursery rows in the garden.

Grasses can also be purchased as seed, though this is only satisfactory if one is growing true botanical species and varieties, since the cultivated varieties of grasses can usually be increased only by division. Seed of ornamental grasses can be obtained by mail order and sometimes from garden centres or nurseries, or from the gardens of friends, but they should never be collected from the wild without the appropriate legal documentation. Growing grasses from seed makes it possible to produce a large number of plants quickly and cheaply. This also makes it possible to select forms that may be superior to those generally grown, though one would have to raise huge numbers to make such a selection.

SITING

As a rule of thumb the true grasses should be grown on poor, well-drained soil in the sun, the sedges in more shaded places in damper, often richer soils, the rushes in moist or marshy ground in sun, the wood rushes in shade, whether wet or dry, and the cat-tails in the sun with their feet in water. There are exceptions, however; for example, the eulalia grasses (*Miscanthus*) will grow in quite wet ground, as will the common reed (*Phragmites australis*). But in general this means that, unless one is highly selective of species and varieties, it is not easy to mix, for example, sedges or rushes with the true grasses.

The siting of grasses is also partly dependent on whether they are warm or cool season growers. Warm season growers revel in warmth and generally need to be planted where they will be in sun nearly all day. Unhappy in cool conditions, they do not start into growth until the temperatures rise at the beginning of summer, thus leaving the ground clear for earlier flowers such as spring and early summer bulbs, including snowdrops, crocus, early and late daffodils and tulips and the early summer camassias.

Cool season growers, by contrast, enjoy the colder weather, usually starting into growth just as soon as the winter loosens its grip but in extreme cases, as with striped bulbous couch grass (*Arrhenatherum elatius* subsp. *bulbosum* 'Variegatum'), starting into growth in autumn and growing fitfully through the winter in mild climates but stopping growth completely in severe winter weather. The downside of this is their dislike of summer heat, many becoming dormant or semi-dormant through much of the summer. At this time they can really let the garden down, looking either as though they are dying or leaving a hole where you think they ought to be. Such problems can be minimized by careful siting. Many cool season growers will grow best and stay looking good for longest if they are grown in shade or semi-shade, which will tend to keep off the worst heat of summer; this is especially true in climates with high summer temperatures. Obviously, if planted at the front of a bed or border the unattractiveness of their summer dormancy will be plainly visible. If planted further back, grasses and other plants that come into season later can spring up to hide their dormancy. The space left in summer by cool season grasses can be taken up by an underplanting of summer-flowering bulbs, such as lilies, summer hyacinth (*Galtonia candicans*) or, if grown in light shade, woodlanders such as *Arisaema*.

THE SUN

It is important to be aware of the position of the sun when siting ornamental grasses, though this is less important with the sedges, rushes and cat-tails. The flowers of miscanthus and pampas grasses, as well as those of the early summer flowering *Cortaderia* species such as *C. richardii*, the Mauritanian rope grass (*Ampelodesmos mauritanica*) and Spanish oat grass (*Stipa gigantea*) take on luminous qualities of breathtaking beauty when seen with the sun shining through them from behind or from beside them, illuminating them against a dark background such as pines or evergreen shrubs. The same applies to grasses with coloured or variegated foliage, especially those with white-variegated leaves such as the striped eulalia grasses but it is less important in those with yellow-striped or zebra-striped leaves, though interesting effects can still be obtained. Grasses whose foliage takes on rich hues in autumn also benefit from having the sun behind them. Indeed, it can help to highlight contrasting colours, the clear yellow of *Panicum virgatum* 'Strictum' as compared with the vinous purplish tones of *P. virgatum* 'Shenandoah', for example. Japanese blood grass (*Imperata cylindrica* 'Rubra'), whose leaves are suffused blood-red by summer, takes on an amazing vibrancy of colour when seen with the sun beyond it.

Consideration should also be given to siting some grasses so that they can be seen from the house in winter, or as one comes and goes to the house. Grasses, after all, contribute more to the garden in winter than other perennials, especially when whitened by a crust of frost. Grasses always look good in association with built structures – whether a house or a terrace, whether stone, brick or concrete – so it is worth siting some near the house. The effectiveness of this combination derives from the contrast between the solidity and bulk of the building and the discrete linearity of the grasses.

When siting grasses it is important to be aware of the sun's position. The sun is seen falling on the grass (*Setaria macrostachya*) in the picture above right, while the same grass is shown with the sun behind it, above left, creating a much more lively effect.

SPACING

The spacing of grasses depends on whether you want the plants to run together in a drift and or to remain as separate individuals, but a rule of thumb is that the distance apart should be half that of the mature height in flower. Such spacing ensures the grasses will grow together as a group and that the competition between their roots will be enough to minimize the growth of competing weeds (the spacing for individual grasses is given in the Gallery of Grasses, pages 54–135). If the aim is to see each plant as an individual, however, the spacing should be the same as the mature height of the plant in flower.

planting and after-care

Where individual grasses are to be slipped into an existing scheme, it is usually sufficient simply to clear the ground of weeds and work the soil to a nice crumbly consistency. Bearing in mind that grasses on the whole are plants of poorer rather than richer soils, it may even be worth impoverishing the soil by the addition of coarse grit or gravel. For larger schemes involving many grasses, or grasses and forbes (non-grass perennials), it is best to prepare the ground well beforehand. It should be cleared of all weeds, especially pernicious perennial weeds like ground elder, bindweed and couch grass, preferably by using a glyphosate weedkiller. You may need to give more than one application, so it is essential to leave plenty of time for further applications. The importance of clearing the ground cannot be over-emphasized. It will be almost impossible to remove pernicious weeds from an extensive planting of grasses, with or without forbes, once it is established. You will then need to prepare individual planting sites (see pictures below).

Since most grasses are sensitive to planting depth, it is important that the hole taken out is big enough to allow for the grass to be planted in the ground to the same depth as it was in the pot: the soil in the pot should be level with the surrounding soil. This is easily checked by presenting the plant in its pot to the

PREPARING FOR PLANTING

THE SINGLE MOST IMPORTANT FACTOR IN THE SUCCESSFUL ESTABLISHMENT OF ANY GRASS IS PREPARATION OF THE GROUND BEFORE PLANTING.

BECAUSE GRASSES ARE PLANTS OF POOR SOILS, IT IS USUALLY NECESSARY TO ADD PLENTY OF COARSE GRIT OR SHARP SAND TO THE SOIL.

MIX SAND AND SOIL TOGETHER WELL, MAKING SURE THAT THE AREA OF THE PLANTING HOLE IS PROPORTIONAL TO THE SIZE OF THE PLANT.

PLANTING OUT

TIP THE GRASS (*MOLINIA CAERULEA* SUBSP. *ARUNDINACEA*) OUT OF ITS POT AND CHECK THAT THE HOLE CAN ACCOMMODATE THE ROOTBALL WITH EASE.

LOOSEN THE ROOTS TO ENCOURAGE THEM TO GROW AWAY STRONGLY. ANY DAMAGE WILL RESULT IN VIGOROUS NEW ROOTS THAT WILL MOVE QUICKLY INTO THE SOIL.

PLANT THE GRASS TO THE SAME DEPTH AS IT WAS IN THE POT, AND PRESS DOWN THE SOIL ALL AROUND IT UNTIL FIRM.

MULCHING STRAIGHT AFTER PLANTING HELPS TO PRESERVE SOIL MOISTURE AND SUPPRESS WEEDS.

hole before planting. Otherwise, grasses can be planted in much the same way as one plants any other sort of perennial. In general it is best to plant in spring when the soil is warming up, though in mild winter climates, such as that of the UK, cool season grasses can just as well be planted in autumn. It is never wise to plant in high summer.

After planting, the grass or grasses will need to be thoroughly watered. If planted in spring, this watering is often sufficient to see them through their first season, but it is essential to keep an eye on them. If they are short of water they will roll their leaves, and you should water them at once.

PLANTING IN CONTAINERS

Many grasses look superb in containers, but it is important to make sure that the container is large enough for the expected growth of the grass, and that it has adequate drainage holes. Cover the drainage holes with shards of broken clay pots or pebbles (see page 146), then partly fill the container with a soil-based potting mix. Position the grass before filling the rest of the container with the growing mix, leaving sufficient space above for watering. If the growing mix does not contain any coarse grit, add no more than a quarter by volume. Peat-based growing mixes, and those based on peat substitutes, generally dry out too quickly for ornamental grasses, and they are difficult to re-wet once dry. Grasses grown in containers will need to be watered far more frequently than grasses in

PLANTING IN POTS

CROCK THE POT WELL, THEN PART-FILL WITH COMPOST MIXED WITH COARSE SAND OR GRIT.

PLANT THE GRASS THEN ADD MORE MIX, KEEPING IT AT THE SAME LEVEL AS IN THE ORIGINAL POT.

WATER THOROUGHLY, RAISE THE POT ON 'POT FEET' OR CROCKS, THEN STAND IN A SHADY PLACE UNTIL THE GRASS (HERE, *PENNISETUM GLAUCUM*) IS RE-ESTABLISHED.

the garden, which is why it is important to ensure good drainage, both by adequately crocking the container, and by ensuring sufficient grit in the growing mix. In hot weather they may need to be watered daily, and should be given a liquid feed at least once a week.

MULCHING AND WEEDING

Mulching the ground after planting can be an effective way to conserve soil moisture and to suppress weed growth. Conserving soil moisture can help newly planted grasses to establish but the mulch needs to be 5cm deep to be effective in suppressing weeds – and this can be a cause of other problems. Many small or young grasses are sensitive to having the mulch piled up too closely around their crowns, and this can induce rots and fungi. Despite this, the benefits of mulching generally outweigh the disadvantages.

The weeding of ornamental grass plantings can present problems since many of the weeds of ornamental grasses are in fact other grasses. While it is easy enough to recognize broad-leaved weeds, the grass weeds may look so like the ornamental species that one is uncertain whether to pull them out or not, especially among young, newly planted grasses that are not yet in flower. You can learn best by experience, but signs to look for are the size and colour of the leaf, the position of the leaf in relation to the culm and the degree of hairiness. Some grasses, particularly the tufted hair grasses (*Deschampsia cespitosa*), drop seed among their own leaves so that seedling tufted hair grasses come up in the midst of the clump, identical to the parent in leaf, but not true to type in flower. Such seedlings are usually spotted only once they flower, and little can be done about them.

MULCHES

MANY MULCHES, INCLUDING BARK CHIPPINGS (ABOVE) MAKE AN ATTRACTIVE SURFACE AGAINST WHICH TO DISPLAY GRASSES.

COARSE GRIT IS ANOTHER SUITABLE MULCH FOR GRASSES. IT HELPS TO KEEP IN THE SOIL MOISTURE AND KEEP OUT WEEDS.

CUTTING DOWN

MANY LARGE ORNAMENTAL GRASSES NEED TO BE CUT DOWN WITH LONG-HANDLED LOPPERS.

LARGER PLANTINGS ARE QUICKLY CLEARED USING AN ELECTRIC HEDGE TRIMMER.

CLEAR AWAY THE PRUNINGS FROM GROOMING OPERATIONS USING A SPRING-TINED RAKE.

GROOMING AND CONTROLLING

One of the great virtues of grasses is that they need relatively little care, but it is essential that they receive what little they need. Provided they have been planted in ground that has been thoroughly cleared of weeds beforehand, spaced reasonably close together and sensibly mulched after planting, little weeding should be needed other than during the annual late-winter purge of the garden. The routine maintenance of grasses consists of an annual clear-up, which is usually carried out in late winter or very early spring; the moment of choice varies with the degree of tidiness required of the garden. The attrition of winter gradually erodes the grasses and by late winter they are starting to disintegrate, creating a wind-blown litter of shredded leaves and culms. There comes a time when the ugliness of this litter is greater than the beauty of the standing stems, and that is the moment to cut them down.

Tall grasses such as the eulalias (*Miscanthus*) should be cut down to about 15cm from the ground, while smaller grasses may be cut closer to the ground. With young plants it is easy enough to cut them down using secateurs or, with smaller grasses, scissors, but with large, well-established clumps and with extensive plantings it may be necessary to use powered hedge trimmers, strimmers or even a chain saw. Only grasses that have turned beige or buff should be cut down.

Evergreen grasses should be groomed by raking the dead leaves out of the clumps. This can be done using a garden rake or, with small grasses, with the fingers. Some people like to set fire to the dry leaves of grasses in late winter and, while this will effectively clear the top growth and even provide some useful potash, it can be dangerous in an urban or suburban garden. Fire can be quite effective at clearing the dead leaves from a clump of Argentinian pampas grass (*Cortaderia*) but little and often is the rule. Fires are frequent, often occurring annually, in the pampa prairies of South America and as there are relatively few leaves to be burned, the fire travels fast and lightly. Problems arise when people, thinking they are following this precedent, set fire to a clump of pampas grass that has not been cleaned of its dead leaves for many years. The fire then burns much more fiercely and may severely damage or even kill the clump.

Once the grasses have been cut down, the trimmings need to be raked up and removed, though on a small scale it is possible to chop them up or shred them for use as a mulch. This is an excellent practice since it returns the dead leaves to the ground around the plant, much as would happen in the wild. While the ground is clear, and before the grasses start into growth again, this is the ideal moment to clear any weeds that have come up. It is quite safe to use glyphosate weedkillers, provided that not a single green leaf can be seen among the stumps of the ornamental grasses or on any of the other plants growing among them. The only other routine maintenance needed is to keep the grasses young and vigorous by dividing and either replanting or transplanting them.

Collect the seeds of grasses by drawing the seedhead between fingers and thumbnail (far left). The seeds of many will germinate quickly if they are sown straight away .

Grass seeds are usually contained in a husk, which is all that remains of the floret as it dries on ripening (left). Remove the husks by winnowing before sowing the seed because they may otherwise become the focus of fungal disease as they decay.

propagating grasses

Annual grasses have to be raised from seed because there is no other way to propagate them, but perennial grasses are usually increased by division since seed-raised plants of named varieties seldom replicate the virtues of the parent.

RAISING FROM SEED

Seed may be bought or collected from the garden. If it is not to be sown immediately, store it over winter in a cool, dry place at a constant temperature: inside a paper bag in a sealed tin kept in the refrigerator is ideal.

Hardy annual grasses are usually grown from seed sown out of doors in late spring where they are to flower; most will then flower from midsummer onwards. Earlier flowering can be achieved by treating these grasses as biennial, sowing seed where it is to flower in late summer. In some gardens annual grasses seed themselves, and all you need do is ensure that they do not seed too freely. When seeds of annual grasses are sown where they are to grow, you could outline the area with sand: then the majority of grass seedlings that come up will be those you have sown, making it easy to spot unwanted seedlings.

Seed of half-hardy annuals is generally best sown in late winter or early spring in trays or pots in a greenhouse or cold frame. Seedlings can be transplanted to individual pots once two or three true leaves have formed, and set out in the garden when large enough, provided the danger of frost is over. Rates of germination vary, some germinating in a week or two, and others taking months, while a few need a period of chilling. If grown under glass, ventilate the seedlings well to prevent damping-off, a fungal infection which can also be reduced by using fungicides.

PROPAGATING SMALL AND LARGE SEED

SCATTER SMALL GRASS SEEDS
THINLY ONTO THE WELL-FIRMED
SURFACE OF A SUITABLY GRITTY
GROWING MIX DESIGNED FOR SEEDS.

COVER THE SEEDS WITH A LAYER OF
SHARP SAND OR GRIT WHICH WILL
HELP TO KEEP THEM IN CONTACT
WITH THE COMPOST.

FIRM THE SURFACE WITH THE
BOTTOM OF A POT OR A TAMPER,
AND WATER FROM UNDERNEATH
UNTIL THE SURFACE IS WET.

LARGE GRASS SEEDS, SUCH AS
THOSE OF *STIPA BARBATA* SHOWN
HERE, NEED TO BE INSERTED
SINGLY, MAKING SURE THEY ARE
THE RIGHT WAY UP.

COVER THE SURFACE OF THE
POTTING MIX WITH A LAYER OF
SHARP SAND OR GRIT TO REDUCE
EVAPORATION.

MOVE SEEDLINGS ON TO INDIVIDUAL
POTS AS SOON AS THEY DEVELOP
TWO TRUE LEAVES AND ALLOW
THEM TO GROW ON UNTIL LARGE
ENOUGH TO PLANT OUT.

Most grass seedlings benefit from a period of hardening off once they are taken out from under glass. Stand them outdoors in a position sheltered from wind and, in summer, shaded from the sun's rays. Young grasses are vulnerable to desiccation on both counts and should be kept watered since no amount of later watering will make up for dryness at the roots when the grasses are young.

DIVIDING AND TRANSPLANTING

Grasses, like all clump-forming perennials, grow out from the centre forming an ever-expanding ring, gradually exhausting the soil in which they are growing. After several or many years the quantity and quality of the flowering declines, and the centre of the clump dies out. The remedy is to divide the clump, which will renew its vigour. With small, tightly clumping grasses such as the fescues, it may be necessary to lift and divide every two or three years, while with larger grasses, such as the eulalias, this need only be done every five to ten years, though some people leave their clumps much longer. A well-established clump of a medium-sized eulalia grass such as *Miscanthus sinensis* 'Flamingo' should yield about five decent new plants after five to ten years growing.

DIVIDING SMALL CLUMPS

MOST GRASSES CAN BE EASILY DIVIDED STRAIGHT FROM THE GARDEN. FIRST, DIG UP THE CLUMP AND SHAKE OFF THE SURPLUS SOIL.

PLACE THE CLUMP ON THE GROUND AND CUT THROUGH THE CROWN WITH A SHARP, STRONG KNIFE.

TEASE THE CLUMP APART WITH YOUR HANDS. THE PROCESS MAY BE REPEATED, PRODUCING SMALLER AND SMALLER DIVISIONS.

CUT DOWN THE TOP GROWTH OF EACH DIVISION, THEN REDUCE THE ROOTS BY A THIRD OF THEIR LENGTH TO STIMULATE NEW ROOT GROWTH.

DIVIDING MATURE CLUMPS

CUT AWAY LARGE PIECES OF THE CLUMP CLEANLY, USING A SPADE, BEFORE LIFTING THEM OUT OF THE GROUND.

THE SIMPLEST METHOD IS THEN TO CUT THE CLUMP INTO SMALLER PIECES WITH A SHARP SPADE.

LARGE CLUMPS MAY HAVE TO BE SPLIT WITH AN AXE TO REDUCE THEM TO MANAGEABLE PIECES.

WHEN THE ROOTS ARE VERY TOUGH, YOU MAY NEED TO USE A BOW SAW TO CUT THROUGH THEM.

With small clumps it is simple enough to dig up the plants and split them, using a trowel or garden fork. The dead parts of the plant from the centre of the clump should be discarded and the old clump replaced by a piece or pieces from the outside, where the clump is growing most vigorously. Mature specimens of large grasses, such as eulalias and pampas grasses (*Cortaderia*), may be too big and heavy to dig up in one piece, in which case they are best divided in the ground into smaller portions, rather like slices of a round cake. Each slice can then be removed on its own. Sometimes it is possible to divide the roots by slicing at them with a sharpened spade, but often the roots of mature grasses are both densely tangled and as hard as oak, so that it may be necessary to use an axe or a bow saw. Once out of the ground, the sections can be planted elsewhere. If they are used to replace the old clump, the exhausted soil should first be replaced with new soil from elsewhere in the garden, or given a little slow-acting fertilizer such as bonemeal.

Dividing and transplanting clumps can be done at the same time as cutting down their top growth, but can also be successful if left until new growth starts to appear. This not only lets you see which parts of the plant are growing most vigorously but actually increases the likelihood of the transplants surviving. The ground to receive the transplants should be well prepared beforehand, as for a shrub or a small tree, and the new plant thoroughly firmed in the ground, then watered in. Ideally, the surrounding ground should be mulched to reduce water evaporation from the soil, and this can be done with either organic or inorganic materials, or with a temporary device such as a mulching mat.

CUTTING AND DRYING

Long before ornamental grasses were considered fit to plant in gardens, their flowerheads and foliage – fresh, dried or dyed – were found in florists' shops and widely used in floral arrangements, treasured for the delicacy of their texture and the subtlety of their colouring. What makes the dried flowers of grasses so desirable is that they look much the same dried as they do fresh, unlike other blooms which tend to drop their showy petals. Moreover, the flowers of grasses, being subtly coloured when fresh, have little colour to lose when dried.

When picking the flowers of grasses the secret of success is to pick them rather earlier than would seem sensible, just as the flowerhead is emerging from the leaves. The very last moment to pick them is when the anthers – the male, pollen-bearing parts of the flowers – appear. By the time pollen grains can be seen, usually conspicuously cream, white or yellow, it is too late for, once pollinated, the seeds will start to develop and, as they ripen, the likelihood that the flower will shatter increases. Once ripe, of course, the seeds drop out and with them most of the floret, leaving only the empty glumes. Even in that eviscerated state, many grasses can still be attractive and long lasting in dried arrangements, especially in winter.

Grasses differ greatly in the alacrity with which the flowers shatter when dried. Those of squirrel-tail grass (*Hordeum jubatum*) shatter so fast that one scarcely has time to take them indoors, and those of ruby grass (*Melinis roseus*), are little better. Both these grasses are best used as fresh flowers and stood in water which needs to be frequently topped up. Most of the warm season growers, and most of the larger grasses, will last for several months once dried, if picked early enough.

The flowers of grasses can be dried quite simply by picking them, tying their stems loosely with string or raffia, and hanging them upside down in a cool, dark, airy place such as a garden shed or garage. Coolness is important, because warmth increases the likelihood of the flowers shattering, and darkness is vital because the colours may fade if exposed to sunlight. The flowers of most grasses dry in 10–14 days, but it is important to check them periodically because, as they dry, the stems shrink and may slip out of the noose holding them together.

Some people like to strip the leaves off their grasses before drying them, and others like to leave them on. It is partly a matter of personal choice and partly depends on the grasses being dried. Some leaves are worth drying in their own right, those of eulalia grasses, for instance, but they may need to be pressed between sheets of absorbent paper to keep them flat, rather than being hung up to dry. The leaves of the maiden grass (*Miscanthus sinensis* 'Gracillimus'), by contrast, are valued in arrangements for their curly character and are best dried attached to the flowering culms.

Hang grasses to dry in a cool, airy place, such as the back of a shed door. Most grasses retain their beauty when dried or in seed.

DISEASES AND PESTS

DISEASES

Ornamental grasses are generally not troubled by bacterial and viral diseases, but fungal pathogens may sometimes cause problems. One of the more important problems is rust, an infection by one of several species of fungi which reveals itself as small, orange- or brown-coloured pustules on the leaves. Minor infections often pass unnoticed, but severe infection can disfigure a plant and reduce its vigour. Striped bulbous oat grass (*Arrhenatherum elatius* subsp. *bulbosum* 'Variegatum') and tufted hair grass (*Deschampsia cespitosa* 'Bronzeschleier') are particularly susceptible. Infections are most likely to occur where grasses are growing too close together, or where there is very little air movement.

Another fungal disease that sometimes occurs is powdery mildew, causing a powdery white deposit on the leaves, again reducing vigour. A leaf spot caused by the fungus *Leptosphaeria* has been identified recently in the USA on *Miscanthus*. Other fungal leaf spots are also occasionally troublesome. In the UK, fungicides containing myclobutanil and penconazole are labelled for the control of rust and powdery mildew on ornamentals. These fungicides will protect against infection and also prevent existing infections becoming more serious; they may also give some control of leaf spots. Proprietary fungicides will also give some control in other countries. However, fungicides can do little once infections have become severe, where the most appropriate action is to cut off and burn affected leaves. Other fungi that occasionally occur include smuts (*Ustilago* spp.) which erupt from infected tissues as masses of dark, powdery spores. Grasses are occasionally infected by the ergot fungus (*Claviceps purpurea*) which also causes ergot in cereals. Infected flowers first exude a sticky honeydew and are then replaced by a dark, hard fungal mass. Plants affected by these fungi should be dug up and burnt promptly, and the ground should not be replanted with the same species, because smut spores and ergots can contaminate the soil.

RUST IS ONE OF THE FEW PROBLEMS TO AFFLICT ORNAMENTAL GRASSES.

PESTS

Slugs and snails can do some damage to grasses, though in general the grasses have sufficient vigour to grow faster than they are being devoured. Seedlings are much more vulnerable, and the sedges are generally more prone to damage than the true grasses. Proprietory remedies are available.

Ants can sometimes be a problem, building their nests in the crown of, and underneath, a grass. There are various proprietory remedies, but they need to be used with caution as some are harmful to plants.

Rabbits are especially partial to the tufted hair grasses (*Deschampsia*), though they seldom eat other grasses down to the ground. The only real remedy is rabbit fencing, which has to be buried in the ground and then turned outwards to prevent the rabbits from digging their way underneath, but such fencing is expensive.

Deer will nibble anything, especially if it is newly planted, but do not usually do a great deal of damage. More damaging are voles, which seem to undergo periodic population explosions. They burrow and will eat the roots of the plants. If necessary, set some mouse traps under the cover of logs or bricks close to where the damage is occuring.

Miscanthus mealybug (*Miscanthiococcus miscanthi*), an Asian native, is becoming a serious pest of miscanthus in some eastern and southern states in America. Like most mealybugs it is a tiny creature, no more than 4mm long, and small enough to be easily overlooked, the more so since infestations occur in the almost non-existent space between leaf sheath and culm. Because of this, infestations are not usually noticed until the plant is showing obvious signs of distress, typically a stunting of growth and a twisting of the flowerheads. Another symptom of infestation is that the stem and stem sheath turn dark red towards the end of the season.

Unfortunately, once the presence of miscanthus mealybug has been confirmed, there is little that can be done to get rid of the infestation. They seem resistant to all known insecticides and cannot be eradicated even by winter burning of the miscanthus clumps, since the mealybugs can overwinter deep down among the bases of the culms. The only real remedy is to burn the whole plant, and not to replant miscanthus in the same place for at least a season. Miscanthus mealybug does not occur at present in the UK.

where to see ornamental grasses

UNITED KINGDOM

Blooms of Bressingham
Bressingham, Diss
Norfolk IP22 2AB
www.bloomsofbressingham.co.uk

Hall Farm Nursery
Vicarage Lane
Kinnerley
Nr. Oswestry
Shropshire SY10 8DH

Hoecroft Plants
Severals Grange
Holt Road, Wood Norton
Dereham, Norfolk NR20 5BL
www.hoecroft.co.uk

Jungle Giants
Ferney
Onibury
Craven Arms SY7 9BJ
www.junglegiants.co.uk

Mozart House Nursery Garden
84 Central Avenue
Wigston Magna, Wigston
Leicesteshire LE18 2AA
 By appointment only
Tel: 0116 288 9548

The Beth Chatto Garden Ltd
Elmstead Market
Colchester
Essex CO7 7DB
info@bethchatto.fsnet.co.uk

The Campbell-Sharp Grassery
Marlborough, Wiltshire
Strictly by appointment only
Tel. 01672 515380

Knoll Gardens
Hampreston, Stapehill
Nr. Wimborne
Dorset BH21 7ND
www.knollgardens.co.uk

The Royal Botanic Gardens
Kew, Richmond
Surrey TW9 3AE.

The Royal Horticultural Society's Garden Rosemoor
Great Torrington
North Devon EX38 8PH

The Royal Horticultural Society's Garden Wisley, Woking
Surrey GU23 6QB

EUROPE

Clara Garden – Casa Rocca Collections
Vivai Bilancioni
Via fermignano 3/7
Bellaria (RN)47813 (RIMINI)
Italy

Karl-Foerster Garten
Amundsenstrasse
Potsdam
Germany

Le Jardin Plume
Le Thil, 76116 Auzouville-sur-Ry
France
lejardinplume@fnac.net

Piet Oudolf
Broekstraat 17
6999 de Hummelo
Holland
www.oudolf.com

USA

Greenlee Nursery
301 Franklin Avenue
Pomona, CA 91766

Kurt Bluemel, Inc.
2740 Greene Lane
Baldwin, MD 21013
www.kurtbluemel.com

Longwood Gardens
US Route 1
PO Box 501
Kennett Square, PA 19348
www.longwoodgardens.org

Manito Park
Spokane,
Washington

Plant Delights Nursery, Inc.
Juniper Level Botanic Gardens
9241 Sauls Road
Raleigh, NC 27603
www.plantdelights.com

The Donald M. Kendall Sculpture Garden
PepsiCo Headquarters
Purchase, New York
(grass garden designed by Russell Page)

CANADA

Free Spirit Nursery
20405 – 32 Avenue
Langley, B.C. V2Z 2C7

where to buy ornamental grasses

UNITED KINGDOM

Hall Farm Nursery
Vicarage Lane, Kinnerley
Nr. Oswestry
Shropshire SY10 8DH
www.hallfarmnursery.co.uk

Hoecroft Plants
Severals Grange
Holt Road, Wood Norton
Dereham
Norfolk NR20 5BL
www.hoecroft.co.uk

John Chambers Wild Flower Seeds
15 Westleigh Road
Barton Seagrave
Kettering
Northamptonshire NN15 5AJ

Knoll Gardens
Hampreston, Stapehill
Nr. Wimborne
Dorset BH21 7ND
www.knollgardens.co.uk

Marchants Hardy Plants
2 Marchants Cottages
Ripe Road, Laughton
East Sussex BN8 6AJ

Monksilver Nursery
Oakington Road
Cottenham
Cambridge CB4 8TW
www.monksilver.com

Mozart House Nursery Garden
84 Central Avenue
Wigston
Leicestershire LE18 2AA
By appointment only
Tel: 0116 288 9548

Pennard Plants
The Walled Gardens
East Pennard
Shepton Mallet
Somerset BA4 6TU
www.pennardplants.com

Phoenix Perennial Plants
Paice Lane
Medstead, Alton
Hampshire GU34 5PR
Greenfarmplants.Marina.
Christopher@Care4free.net

The Big Grass Company
Hookhill Plantation
Woolfardisworthy East
Black Dog
Nr. Crediton
Devon EX17 4RX
www.big-grass.co.uk

The Beth Chatto Gardens Ltd.
Elmstead Market
Colchester
Essex CO7 7DB
info@bethchatto.fsnet.co.uk

The Ornamental Grass Nursery
Church Farm, Westgate
Rillington
Malton
North Yorkshire YO17 8LN
www.ornamentalgrass.co.uk

The Plantsman's Preference
Lynwood, Hopton Road
Garboldisham
Diss
Norfolk IP22 2QN
www.plantpref.co.uk

The Wisley Plant Centre
RHS Garden Wisley
Woking
Surrey GU23 6QB
Tel. 01483 211 113
www.rhs.org.uk/Wisley

EUROPE

Bambous de Planbuisson
Rue Montaigne
24480 Le Buisson de
Cadouin
France
www.planbuisson.com

Crea' Paysage
Lannenec, 56270 Ploemeur
France
creapaysage@wanadoo.fr

Didier Marchand
La Cordonnaie
35560 Bazouges La Perouse
France

Le Jardin Plume
Le Thil, 76116 Auzouville-
sur-Ry
France
lejardinplume@fnac.net

Piet Oudolf
Broekstraat 17
6999 de Hummelo
Holland
www.oudolf.com

USA

Andre Viette Farm & Nursery
Route 1, Box 16
Fishersville, VA 22939

Carroll Gardens
444 East Main Street
PO Box 310
Westminster, MD 21157
www.carrollgardens.com

Greenlee Nursery
301 E. Franklin Avenue
Pomona, CA 91766

Kurt Bluemel, Inc.
2740 Greene Lane
Baldwin MD 21013
www.kurtbluemel.com

Limerock Ornamental Grasses
R.D. 1, Box 111-C
Port Matilda, PA 16870
www.limerockgrasses.com

New England Bamboo Company
5 Granite Street
Rockport, MA 01966
www.newengbamboo.com

Plant Delights Nursery, Inc.
Juniper Level Botanic Gardens
9241 Sauls Road
Raleigh NC 27603
www.plantdelights.com

Wayside Gardens
1 Garden Lane, Hodges,
SC 29695
www.waysidegardens.com

CANADA

Blue Stem Nursery
1946 Fife Road
Christina Lake
BC, V0H 1E3
mneale@bluestem.ca

further reading

Darke, Rick, *The Color Encyclopedia of Ornamental Grasses*, Timber Press, Portland, Oregon, 1999

Grounds, Roger, *The Plantfinder's Guide to Ornamental Grasses*, David and Charles, Newton Abbot, Devon,1998

Oaks, A.J., *Ornamental Grasses and Grasslike Plants*, Van Nostrand Reinhold, New York, 1990

Oehme, Wolfgang and James van Sweden, *Bold Romantic Gardens*, Acropolis Books, Reston, Virginia, 1990

Ondra, Nancy J., *Grasses, Versatile Partners for Uncommon Garden Design*, Garden Art Press, Woodbridge, Suffolk, 2002

Ottesen, Carole, *Ornamental Grasses, The Amber Wave*, McGraw-Hill, New York, 1989

Oudolf, Piet (with Michael King), *Gardening with Grasses*, Frances Lincoln, 1998

acknowledgments

AUTHOR'S ACKNOWWLEDGMENTS

The author wishes to thank the many people who have helped to turn the initial idea into a marvellous book, particularly Jane O'Shea and the team at Quadrille. They have been a joy to work with, especially my meticulous and patient editor Carole McGlynn, and Paul Welti whose struggle with the conflicting claims of text and pictures has resulted in such elegant and approachable pages. My thanks also to Susanne Mitchell of the Royal Horticultural Society who proposed the book in the first place, and to Simon Maughan for seeing it through.

My particular thanks go to: Andrew Lawson whose beautiful pictures adorn these pages; the owners of nurseries and gardens who kindly permitted their plants and gardens to be photographed, especially Neil Lucas and the Knoll Gardens, Hampreston, Dorset, the Royal Botanic Gardens, Kew, the Royal Horticultural Society's Gardens at Wisley and Rosemoor, Messrs. Ball-Colgrave, West Adderbury, Oxford, the University Botanic Garden, Oxford; and the owners of many private gardens in the United Kingdom, Europe and the United States of America.

I am also grateful to Sarah Cuttle, who took the practical pictures, and to both Marina Christopher of Phoenix Perennial Plants and Neil Lucas at The Knoll Gardens whose expert knowledge and help made Sarah's pictures so accurately informative.

Finally, I should like to thank the many nursery people and other colleagues, both at home and abroad, who have shared with me their knowledge and love of ornamental grasses – and often their plants – over the years. To all of them I shall be eternally grateful.

PHOTOGRAPHIC ACKNOWLEDGMENTS

All photography by Andrew Lawson except that by Sarah Cuttle on pages: 16–25 (excluding pictures on pages 19 and 21, inset, by Andrew Lawson) and 136–153.

6-7 designers: Oehme and van Sweden; 11 Hestercombe Gardens; 12-13 designers: Oehme and van Sweden; 14-15 Pensthorpe Waterfowl Park, Norfolk, designer: Piet Oudolf, Hummelo; 26-27 Sticky Wicket, Dorset: designer Pam Lewis; 28 designers: Biddy Bunzl & James Fraser; 30-31 Sticky Wicket, Dorset, designer: Pam Lewis; 31 designer: Christopher Bradley-Hole; 32 designer: Piet Oudolf, Hummelo; 33 left designer: Tom Stuart-Smith; 34 designers: Oehme and van Sweden; 35 Bury Court, designer: Christopher Bradley-Hole; 39 designer: Tom Stuart-Smith; 43 designer Tom Stuart-Smith; 44-5 designer: Tom Stuart-Smith; 48 Lady Farm, Chelwood, Somerset; 49 Pensthorpe Waterfowl Park, Norfolk, designer: Piet Oudolf; 50 designers: Oehme and van Sweden; 52 above RHS Gardens, Wisley; 52 below designers: Oehme and van Sweden; 53 designer: Tom Stuart-Smith; 104 below designer: Piet Oudolf, Hummelo; 109 above RHS Gardens, Wisley; 109 below Royal Botanic Gardens, Kew.

index